GW00630984

INSIGHT OUT

Christa Pearce

Mardibooks
Bringing WRITERS to READERS

INSIGHT OUT

Christa Pearce

'If you take from this book what you feel is right, the book has served its purpose.'

First published in paperback 2012 by ***mardibooks***
This edition published 2012 by ***mardibooks***
www.mardibooks.com

ISBN 978-1-909227-04-0

A CIP catalogue record for this book is available from the British Library.

Typeset by flamin ape ltd
Printed and bound by CPI Group (UK) Ltd, Croydon, CR0 4YY

Mardibooks
Bringing WRITERS *to* READERS

PUBLISHER'S NOTE

The publisher has used its best effort in preparing this book and the information provided herein by the author is provided 'as is'. ***mardibooks*** (Circa 1 Media Ltd) makes no representation of warranties with respect to the accuracy or completeness of the contents of this book and shall in no event be liable for any misrepresentation, loss or damage, including but not limited to special, incidental, consequential, or other damage, to any individual or institution.

AUTHOR'S NOTE

I have gained permission from all subjects, where practicably possible, for the inclusion of their histories in this work, and preserved people's anonymity where they have requested it.

Contents

Foreword

Using real life case histories, this book gives insightful information into why we suffer food addictions and allergies and how to change that. What we are all aiming for is effective and efficient mobility and an inquisitive mind, throughout our lives.

Each case history addresses different issues: how to feed yourself and what happens when you don't; how muscles and trigger points containing negative emotions can be released; how cranial sacral techniques help to release shock from the system; how telepathy can be experienced and understood; how different illnesses may actually have their origin in another life. It addresses Karma and how the identification of it has helped many people. It also highlights the real danger of taking drugs and their long term effect on emotions.

Telepathy, healing and visions are part of the author's experiences during treatments. Christa encourages self-sufficiency and self-reliance. Each case history carries with it its own learning message, not only for the patient but for the therapist as well. This book is written for people with existing conditions in order for them to understand the whys and wherefores of their own cases and what to do about them. While the bereaved will gain understanding and comfort, it also makes captivating reading for anyone who is interested in life, particularly therapists.

To protect patients, names and locations have been changed. Consent has been given to publicise each of these stories in order to help others to understand their suffering and how to go about helping themselves.

The book covers my background, presents and analyses my fear of death from the age of five and explains how I not only overcame it, but how I now know, rather than merely believe, due to these case histories, that there is only a physical death. The real us, our spirit, is very much alive and can never die.

Preface

'When one door shuts, another opens'

Set in my way of thinking until my mid-thirties, I was content with being the mother of two children and a housewife. My husband then persuaded me to study physical therapy in order to help him in his flourishing practice. Eventually, reluctantly, and believing initially that I couldn't study further at my age, I agreed.

It was two years into being a physical therapist, after passing all the relevant examinations, that I really began to understand the underlying qualities of my profession.

Deep tissue massage not only relaxes muscles. It tends to balance the functioning of all organs in the body and the mind as well. The blood and lymph nodes supply and stimulate the nervous system so that tension in body and mind melt away.

I noticed that during treatment people started opening up, expressing their inner feelings and deep-seated emotions. Trigger points within tight muscles not only contain waste products but can harbour deep emotions such as anger or sadness. In fact our emotions may often originate in the mind but they are stored in many areas of our physical body, mainly in the buttocks, between the shoulder blades and the neck and shoulders.

Healing, through the laying on of hands, taught me to feel the vibrations of different energies, such as static energy in a person with migraine, severe headaches or even a tumour.

I found stroke patients experienced a hypnotic state when I massaged their limbs. It happened so often that I was compelled to study hypnotherapy and psychotherapy and eventually studied for a BSc (Hons.) in Psychology. I also found cranial therapy an important tool in my work.

With hindsight, I have learned more from patients' reactions to therapy than from any books. It can be compared to the difference between passing a driving test and experiencing the open road over time. Each patient reacts differently to therapy and will often need different treatments for the same condition.

I tend to treat the person as a whole; body, mind and spirit. Our life force is an energy, and energies cannot die. They just get displaced. I see us as a spirit within a body, the brain being our computer, operating an unconscious and conscious mind. Most illnesses start in the mind through our attitudes towards certain circumstances. Negativity can lead to physical illness via tension and stress. A positive person generally heals much faster than a downhearted one.

We have free will and we can change our attitudes towards situations. One of my favourite proverbs is: 'The most important thing that anybody will ever tell you, is what you tell yourself.' A Chinese proverb. We have the final say in the matter, and we do tend to act on it. 'Whatever we do to others, good or bad, we do to ourselves.' It's the intention behind the act that counts the most. I also believe what we sow is what we reap. If you carry out acts in your life with unconditional love, it will lead to contentment and peace in every thing you do.

For our spirit to express itself best, we need a healthy mind and body, a wholesome diet, creative hobbies, exercise, healthy and effective breathing, and a positive outlook.

1 My Belief, Faith And Knowledge

Within the first ten years as a therapist I found myself treating the physically ill, some with paralysis, some with psychosomatic conditions and the mentally sick. I learned about healing using unconditional love, and I worked with cranial therapy.

Mrs. M., an 80 year old lady, taught me about spirituality. Most of her valuable thoughts came straight from her guide, an inner voice. She emphasised the importance of getting the foundations right. The longer the learning process continues, the deeper the foundations will be. I'll never forget her saying, 'A house without foundations is vulnerable and can easily collapse.'

Eventually I reached a stage in my spiritual progression when I did not just believe: I knew. The evidence was shown to me again and again. There is an afterlife. Many of my volunteers have given extensive evidence of it during past life regressions. I have even witnessed miracles. There is no doubt in my mind about the soul living on.

I understand it in the following way. We are a spirit with a body. The mind consists of two parts, the conscious and the unconscious, which are both part of the soul. The brain can be seen as our physical computer. When we leave our body behind, both parts of our mind become our complete consciousness. At this point we know everything about ourselves, including all our experiences, not only in this life, but in all our former existences.

My understanding is, now, that our real home is on the other side. That is where we come from and where we will return to when our time is up. There we will still continue to improve ourselves. We will then have the chance to view the life we lived on planet earth. We will learn to understand how we influenced other people; how we conducted ourselves and how they saw us. From our faults we can learn the most. Some mistakes can be rectified on the other side. Some need earthly conditions, which means they have to be re-enacted in a future life, possibly as a victim.

At a later date, when the time is right, we may have physically to experience the ill-treatment we inflicted on somebody else. We may become a born victim. A victim always needs a persecutor. These two will find each other. Ultimately forgiveness plays a major part; either we have to forgive somebody else for what they have done or haven't done, or what we blame them for. Forgiving ourselves is probably the most difficult task to achieve. We are often too hard on ourselves.

After we have inspected our life's journey, with the help of a light being on the other side, we will probably know where we have gone wrong. The emotions we will take with us to the other world, guilt, anger, hate, frustration and others, will need to be addressed eventually, or they will stand in the way of our further spiritual development.

To overcome our self-constructed framework of challenges, I would go as far as to suggest that we probably pick our future parents, in addition to all the other problems we have to face in order to grow.

2 Straight From Heaven

This actually happened in one of my sessions:

I gave a four month pregnant woman a gentle, uplifting massage. After the treatment I put my hands above her slightly swollen stomach. I always ask for permission first. I then sent unconditional love from my heart chakra through the arms into my palms. I could feel my energy amalgamating with the energy of the baby, although I did not touch the stomach. The baby responded by kicking vigorously, so the mum-to-be told me.

I then closed my eyes and concentrated on the baby, asking it for a little message for its mum, anything that came to mind, even just a thought.

Suddenly I felt the shadow of a grown up person alongside me, introducing itself as the spirit of the baby. Then it asked me telepathically, 'Do you want to know when I will move in permanently?'

It explained how one could compare having a baby with building a house. 'First you find a building site. In our case I find a suitable mum. When that is established, I become connected to the embryo, a bit like laying the first brick when building a house. All the time my real home is still on, what you would call, the *other side*.

The baby's spirit continued, 'I am always connected with the growing foetus. It is exciting to see the body of the baby shaping up and its little fingers and toes forming. Comparing that with a building site, you would see the walls being constructed and you'd probably start recognizing the kitchen area.

'Eventually when the house is built to perfection, only then do you move in. This is exactly what happens when the baby is big enough and fully formed. At birth I move in permanently. That means my new home, while on earth, is within the baby. I am the baby.

'My conscious mind, consisting of consciousness and unconsciousness, together on the other side only, becomes partly the new conscious mind of the baby which is more or less empty and needs to be filled with all the experiences of growing up and ageing.

'The other part becomes the baby's unconscious mind. As you know, the unconscious mind contains all the knowledge of previous existences. It stays in the unconscious until I, as the baby, return to my real home, on the other side. Then the newly experienced consciousness will be added to unconscious knowledge. They will then both become one consciousness again.'

3 My Childhood Beliefs

From an early age my Mother taught me how to pray. It proved very valuable at different times in my life. She explained to me that when we die we go to heaven. That was fine with me, although I often wondered why that dead bird still lay on the ground and didn't go anywhere.

Apparently I was not the only one. I read in Reader's Digest about a little boy going for a walk with his father along the beach. When he saw a dead seagull on the ground, his father urged him not to worry as, he said, the bird had gone to heaven. After thinking about it for a while, the little boy asked whether God had thrown it back again.

At the age of four the thought of going to heaven sounded good to me, and what my Mum said was always right. This was about to change.

I found myself watching an old-fashioned funeral. There were black horses, a black decorated hearse and a coffin on top with lots of flowers. As we lived in a tiny village in Germany, everyone knew everyone else. Many people were watching the procession to the cemetery. I was puzzled by what was going on and asked a ten year old boy next to me what they were all doing. He then told me bluntly that another boy's father had died and that he was in that box to be put into a hole in the cemetery. There and then I corrected him, saying that his Dad had gone to heaven. He told me not to be stupid.

'They put the coffin in the hole.'

I did not believe him, but I needed to be sure. So off I went to the cemetery where I saw the hole dug. I was devastated. My belief was shattered. Strangely I never discussed it with my mother, but kept it to myself. The damage it created lasted until my late thirties.

I developed a phobia of anything to do with dying: death, coffins and cemeteries with holes in the ground. When I saw a funeral procession I instantly looked away and stopped breathing until it had gone. At the same time I was desperately searching for some evidence of an afterlife. Whenever I was able to read the paper, I scanned through it. Sometimes there was something mentioned on the subject, but nobody was ever sure.

At the age of twenty-one I came to London as a student. I eventually married an Englishman and when I was twenty-six years old we moved into a new house. At that point money was short and I was looking for a part time job in the evening. I ended up in an old people's home looking after the women. It was totally different from my usual office job. I had studied Economics and Business.

Strangely I much preferred working with people, looking after them and helping them rather than dealing with paperwork. We had fun and sometimes we had sad times. Generally I learned much about life from these women. I discovered that people positive earlier in life stay positive later in life. They handle situations much more constructively. With negative people it was the opposite. Positive people would even heal more quickly.

There was only one situation I could not master. When somebody died I could not be near that person. When the undertaker came to the door to bring the coffin, I was always hiding somewhere. I felt such a coward.

4 My First Vision

Eventually I began to work in the community. On one particular morning about thirty years ago, at 8.30 am, I went shopping in a well-known store. The shop had just opened when I entered with my trolley through the big glass entrance. All the tills were still deserted. As I advanced a few steps into the shop I saw a man lying on the floor and another person trying to revive him. I guessed it might be the manager who was giving first aid to the man.

Instantly I felt myself go rigid. I needed to get past them. Shaking like a leaf, I managed not to look. I aimed straight ahead walking the length of the long bread counter. Eventually I had to come back the same way to get to the fruit and vegetable area. I had to walk towards the man on the floor again. At a glance I could see that he was face upwards and appeared deep purple. The other person had left him and I then realised that he was now lifeless, was probably phoning for the ambulance.

I was now almost next to the dead person. Looking straight ahead I faced the glass door. What I witnessed then I could not understand: outside the door stood the doorman, looking into the cloudy sky. He looked quite bored. I wondered what he was doing outside and whether he was supposed to be there in such circumstances. I also thought: English people are funny. They don't even care if somebody is dead on the floor in front of them. The doorman must have seen the dead man on the floor inside the shop. I also wondered how German people would have behaved in such a situation; surely they would have stared at him.

At that point I turned away from the front door. I left the doorman outside and the dead person behind me. I approached the fruit and veg department and heard a lady say to her colleague, 'Jo the doorman has just died.' I asked the lady whether they had two doormen. I knew the doorman well, the one I saw outside. She said they only had the one, Jo.

I left my trolley in the grocery department and went back to the glass front door. There was nobody outside now, and when I looked back behind me I saw that the dead man was Jo, the doorman.

Thinking that I was losing my mind, and seeing things that were not there, I abandoned my shopping and went home. I had no explanation for this weird happening that I had experienced, but at the same time I didn't doubt what I had seen.

Seven years later I got the answer to this episode. I was on the way to Blackpool where I was attending a course in physical therapy. In Euston Station I felt compelled to buy a book to read on the three hour train journey. Earlier in my life I would read many books, but now that I had two children and was studying there was not enough time. Nevertheless I had this urge to buy the book. My attention was drawn to the end of the bookshelf and I was compelled to buy one particular title.

On the train I then realised I had picked up a book about the medium Doris Stokes, concerning her life story. As she was completely new to me, I was intrigued by what I was reading.

When Doris was seven years old her mother had put her to bed one summer's evening. It was warm outside, so the windows were open. Suddenly she heard a commotion further down the road. She saw from the window that there was a house on fire. Immediately she ran out in her pyjamas and went to see what was going on. When she ran back her mother caught her and told her off. Doris asked her mother about the man she had seen, who was severely burned and lying on a stretcher. Her mother told her it was the owner of the house, who had died. Doris disagreed, certain that he was still all right and that she had seen him walking behind the stretcher. She asked the question again, only to be given the same answer. When she disagreed once more, she was told off and ordered back to bed.

I then realised what I had seen in that store: the spirit of the deceased person drifting away from his body, unaware that he had passed over, and still doing his duty.

I had a similar thing happen when I was forty-five.

5 Another Vision

One sunny morning in June, about 15 years ago, my friend Marion and I set off to Bournemouth by car. We were soon driving along on a long empty stretch of the M3 doing about 70 miles an hour. My friend was chatting cheerfully and we were having fun. Suddenly I noticed somebody close behind us. I took another look in my rear mirror. Yes, there was a small white Fiesta barely a metre behind us, its driver in the grip of road rage. How dangerous to be that close to another car at that speed!

I decided to get out of his way and indicated left. Before I actually went into the inside left lane, I took another glance in my rear mirror to see whether he was annoyed with me. I could see him very clearly. He had a round face, his hair was combed back neatly and I noticed that it was receding. He looked amused, on the point of laughing. I could not understand why. If I was in his way, what was so funny about it? I finally came to the conclusion that he might fancy me, even though he had only seen me from the back.

Once in the inner lane I waited for the white car to pass. Nothing happened. My friend was still chatting away and hadn't noticed anything. I looked into my side mirror and could not see the car anymore. I took another look in my rear mirror. Nothing! Where was he? I came to the conclusion that he must have had an accident in that short span of time. But whom had he collided with? There was nobody other than us in front of him. The motorway was deserted, just a long stretch of three lanes. The car had vanished.

I asked my friend, 'Is there any traffic behind us?'

'No,' she answered after checking it out.

I asked her, 'What about in the front?

'No,' she answered again.

'Have another look behind us.'

'No, there are no cars behind us.' She became impatient.

'Are you sure?' I persisted.

'What is the matter with you? There is no traffic anywhere!'

I told her what I had seen, a white car with a man driving it, close behind us, who had suddenly disappeared, along with his car. Concluding that he must have had an accident, I wondered about phoning the police, but found myself held back by the improbability of the story.

My friend asked me details about the look of the man. As I described him in detail, she went white, staring at me like I was mad. She finally told me that this description was her husband who had died ten years ago. I told myself that she had probably wished him back. People do that sometimes and make up the story to make themselves feel better. So I decided to stop discussing the episode any further.

Once in Bournemouth I forgot the incident. I later took my friend home to her house. While I was having a cup of tea she fetched some photographs. I realised the same car I had seen on the motorway, and the same man inside it. It was my friend's husband and their white Fiesta.

It all made sense now. If Marion had seen her husband herself instead of me, she probably would have screamed and we might have had an accident. So he must have showed himself to me knowing that when he vanished I would tell her. The whole thing seemed to have amused him greatly, judging by his laughter.

I did not know that objects like this car could appear as visions. I always thought that only ghosts manifested themselves.

6 Healing Works In Many Ways

The lady with Parkinson's

When I had my children, I could only work in the evening in the old people's home, and at weekends, as these were the only times my husband could look after our baby son. I had to bath the ladies, dress them, put them to bed, help feeding them and give them their daily medication. I particular enjoyed looking after them at these times.

One Sunday afternoon I had just started my duty, and there was nobody else working with me at the time. First of all I checked whether all the women in my care were all right. I entered the library where most of them sat in their armchairs facing each other. I observed that some were asleep and that some were watching me. One lady who was actually suffering from Parkinson's disease sat very uncomfortably in the corner of her chair. It looked as if she might slide out of it any moment. She had her mouth half open and saliva was dribbling down her chin. Tears were continuously running down her face, but there was no sobbing, no sound. As I went closer to her, another woman opposite complained that the crying and dribbling had been going on for ages and was getting on her nerves.

As I was not a trained nurse or a therapist, just an office worker, I wondered what to do with the lady. It was impossible to lift her out of her chair. She was stone cold and absolutely rigid. Then came the thought that she might need to be warmed up, so I put her into a wheelchair by swinging her, in the sitting position, from one chair to another. Then I ran a warm bath and gently lowered her into it. I had learned the skill of moving immobile people without hurting myself.

Once in the bath, I took a bowl, filled it with some of the bathwater and emptied it over her upper body to warm her up. After a while it became a bit monotonous, so I started singing to myself, still pouring the water over her. Then I thought I might as well sing a song that the lady might know. 'Maybe it's because I'm a Londoner' came to mind, as this was always a popular tune with the women in the home. As I sang it Mrs. H. Suddenly attempted a few high-pitched notes herself. She had been rigid and unable to make a sound before. The more I sang and warmed her up, the more she started to get in tune. Suddenly we were both singing it. It was as if the rigidity had melted away and a completely different person had emerged. She started chatting and told me about her three marriages. What a story! We both laughed because she had quite a sense of humour.

I suggested getting out of the bath, putting on her best clothes, doing her hair just the way she liked and then walking back to the library. She did not need her wheelchair anymore. She walked beautifully, without help. As we reached her former seat, the lady opposite her was amazed and wanted to know what medication I had given her.

Looking back now, I realise I wasn't the only one involved in the lady's improvement. Someone had told me, through telepathy, what to do. In hindsight, I understood that this had happened many times already in my life. I will explain it later in the book.

7 Life Is A Hard But Effective Teacher

From working in the old people's home I went on to work in the community. Both my children were going to school now. There was never enough time in the day to do all the jobs such as looking after the family and to work full time. One way or another one manages, sometimes with much stress, fatigue and tears, as most mothers know. I always thought that I was fulfilled and happy, looking after family, house and garden as well as earning the much-needed extra money, though my husband had a good job as an engineer at the time.

Then things went wrong. At least that was how I saw it at the time. Both my parents died within three years of one another. I felt like an orphan although I was thirty-three years old. Insecurity, mixed with loneliness and fading energy due to my bad diet, plagued me. I could not sleep at night and my emotions were in turmoil. Needless to say our marriage was suffering as well.

A few years went by and my husband passed his examinations to become an osteopath. He had studied for a few years whilst working in his other job and had finally made it.

As we were living in a terraced house it was necessary to move into a bigger place, where he could set up his surgery. For the moment my husband managed to work in our sitting room but it proved difficult for both the children and me.

We decided to make a positive move and saw our bank manager. As we weren't exactly certain what we should do, the manager asked me what it was that I really wanted. I looked at him, puzzled. Then I told him I wanted to live in a big house and work with my husband. It just came out. Even as I said it, I thought how stupid the idea was. We did not have anything like the kind of money we would need for a bigger house.

The bank manager advised us to go home, find the house and come back. They'd sort the money out. So we went home, but thought how hopeless it all was.

When we arrived home I found the local 'Informer' newspaper on the doorstep. Instinctively I had a quick look at the property page and fixed my eyes on one corner house. It had plenty of parking space, a large front garden, and was… twice as expensive as the price of our own house. My husband, nevertheless, liked its aspect and location.

At that point, Mrs. M., an 80 year old lady, who was a medium, unknown to my husband who would have been unnerved by her history, came for her appointment. She had injured herself in a fall on a bus. After treatment, I made her a cup of tea and she asked me if we were moving into a double fronted house. I looked surprised and replied we had been thinking about it. Then I showed her the paper with the corner house. She became quite excited, 'That's the one! I saw it in my mind. You will move into that house!' Of course I did not believe her.

By now you will know what's coming. After a few difficulties with the mortgage falling through, and my husband breaking his arm playing rugby just before we were due to move, we made it. We have been here in this house for twenty-five happy and eventful years now.

My husband became very busy. He needed help and persuaded me to start studying again. I thought I was too old at thirty-eight. While I was still working for the Council in the community I started studying, as well as helping my husband and looking after the children. There were the household chores as well as the cleaning and gardening to be done. Needless to say, I felt, and behaved, like a zombie.

I started with 'Health and Beauty Therapy' but did not feel comfortable with de-hairing people and many other less than joyful areas of my work. What I did enjoy however was massage and helping people. So in the next two years I passed remedial massage, advanced massage, then after the third year, manipulative therapy. I stopped studying any further as it became mechanical and I have my roots more in feeling with people.

At that point various stroke patients phoned me independently. They found my advertisement in 'Yellow Pages' and wanted me to visit them. I had never worked with paraplegics before and certainly had not advertised for them. I therefore found it very strange that they all wanted me at the same time, independently. Later I realised that things have occurred in categories like this throughout my life. A few years later, when I qualified in Abnormal Psychology at Birkbeck College, many psychotics phoned me for a massage: I had not advertised for them, but I understood what caused their problems.

I found not for the first time that too much sugar had made their condition much worse.

8 Story Of Mr. H.

Mr. H., 65 years old, suffered from paralysis due to a stroke. The right side of his body, his face, arm, side, leg and foot were severely affected. As the motor nerves were impaired he could feel but could not move a great deal. After a certain length of hospital treatment, it was explained to him that he had to learn to live with it. Any further improvement was not to be expected.

To keep muscle tone and circulation going, I massaged Mr. H. Once a week in his own home. Some days he could move better than others, often related to how mentally agitated or anxious he felt.

One particular morning he had an emotional upset and as a result his paralysed, usually limp arm, became completely stiff. The elbow was bent at 90 degrees and the whole arm was rigid. No matter how we tried, we could not move it out of this position.

I wondered what I could do in order to ease the muscles of his arm. I remembered that we had learned in a healing workshop how to do exercises in the mind. I asked Mr. H., who was resting on my portable couch in his sitting room, to close his eyes and realised the following, as I talked him through it:

'Imagine your right arm is completely healthy, warm and comfortably resting by your side. Imagine that your arm is light, energetic and movable, just as it was before the stroke.

'With your next breath you are starting to raise your arm easily and effortlessly off the couch. Your arm stays extended to your fingertips throughout the exercise. As you breathe gently and normally, you are lifting your arm high and higher. Your fingertips are pointing to the ceiling. Feel the stretch in your ribs, in the muscles of your arm and in the fingers. Now stretch your extended arm as far upwards as you can until it is parallel with the side of your head.'

As I talked Mr. H. Through this routine I actually did not watch him at all, neither had I assisted him in any way. In order to get the feel for the exercise myself I copied exactly what I told him to do. I paid attention only to my own arm, as I needed to talk him through this as realistically as possible.

When I finally turned my attention to him I realised in amazement that Mr. H.'s upper arm had lifted sideways to 90 degrees, yet his elbow was still in the same rigid bent position. Beforehand he could not move any part of the arm or shoulder at all.

Somehow the motor nerve route had found a pathway which allowed him to move that part of his arm using his imagination as reality. When he opened his eyes and saw the position his paralysed arm was in, he called out, 'How did I get there?'

'You tell me,' I said. I was both puzzled and pleased.

I let him do the exercise a few times running. Every time we had the same result. It left me with the conclusion that the mind must have an unimaginable power over the body, both positively and negatively.

9 It Happened Before I Ever Understood Or Trained In Hypnosis

Mr. G., a 60 year old gentleman who came to me, suffered from paralysis due to a stroke. He was so severely affected on his left side that he could not stand on his own and had to be helped onto my portable couch. I visited *him* at home.

Mr. G. had an unusual habit. He could not shut his eyes gently for any length of time. If he was asked to close his eyes, he would tightly squeeze his eyelids together and almost immediately open them again. Therefore he was now unable to sleep, so his family told me.

In the beginning I visited the gentleman three times a week to work on his blood circulation, tone his wasted muscles and to exercise the affected joints gently and passively in order to give him more mobility.

One day, after about two months of treatment, Mr. G. Became so relaxed that he actually fell asleep throughout the entire massage. I was happy at this achievement, but Mr. G. Was not pleased at all. I could not understand why. Later I learned, by chance, that there were so many undercurrents within the family and his mistrust was so great, that he hadn't ever dared to shut his eyes. Also leaving his eyes open managed to take the attention away from his plight. Unfortunately, two heart attacks and one stroke were probably the penalty.

Each successive massage session Mr. G. Went to sleep much more quickly, always against his will. Every time he was more upset and anxious about going to sleep.

Then one day I began massaging his 'bad' arm. He still had some feeling in it, as only the motor nerves were affected, which meant he could not move the limbs himself. Almost instantly he begged me to help him sit up. I helped him up and asked if he was breathing all right. He assured me he was and that he was in no pain.

'What do you want to sit up for?' I probed.

In a very worried tone he pleaded, 'I don't want to go to sleep.'

I finally reassured him to his satisfaction that he wouldn't go to sleep during the course of our proposed chat.

I had to come up with something quickly to stem his panic and told him of my dream the previous night. In it, I was driving my car when the traffic lights suddenly changed to red and before I knew it I jumped the lights. A policeman saw the incident and gave me a ticket.

At that moment, while I was still massaging the same arm, Mr. G. Lifted his good arm. As he was signalling with that hand for me to be cautious and at the same time verbally warning me, his arm dropped and he seemed suddenly lifeless.

I had an overwhelming feeling of terror. I thought Mr. G. Had died on my couch. I was thinking of taking his pulse while I was still massaging the same arm. Then I realised that Mr. G. was breathing very deeply and evenly, just as if he was in a deep sleep. 'How can anyone fall asleep in the middle of an action and a word?' I asked myself.

Strangely I was compelled to continue massaging Mr. G.'s arm. Many thoughts went through my head at once. One of them was the question, 'What do I do next?' Although I had never seen hypnosis before nor did I know anything about it, I had the feeling that he was hypnotised.

'*Test him*,' I seemed to hear, telepathically.

'How?' I wondered.

'*Talk to him*!'

So I started whispering, but got no response. I talked more and more loudly. No response. Then I had a brainwave to tell him something constructive.

'Your arms and legs are feeling warmer and lighter. You are feeling better and better.'

I thought it a good idea to instruct him to do something useful. But still no response. I was convinced he couldn't hear me but wondered whether he would respond to positive instructions. Then like an enlightenment it came to me, *Make him do something. Be precise*!

'You are wiggling your toes now! You are wiggling your toes now!' I shouted. He instantly wiggled the toes on his 'good' foot. I could not believe the success.

My next instruction was, 'You are wiggling the toes on your 'bad' foot now!'

I said it twice again. Everything was quiet. Then suddenly Mr. G. Jerked violently with both legs. It made me jump. I realised he was trying to obey my last suggestion, but could not quite manage it as I was addressing the paralysed side.

All the time I was still massaging Mr. G's same arm. It felt almost like an unsaid instruction not to stop the massaging. I later learned that I had used the hypnotic touch. You can use all five senses to hypnotise a subject.

I noticed that my hour was up and I had to go home for my next appointment. It was necessary to wake Mr. G. Up, but how? Something made me aware that I had to stop my arm massage to sever the connection between us. Realising that I had to tell him to wake up, I moved closer to him. My face was barely ten inches from his face. As I looked at him I suggested, 'in a minute you will be waking up.' No response. I became concerned. 'When you wake up, you will be happy.' Still no response. Then came the thought, '*Be precise*'. I called out, 'You are waking up now!'

Mr. G. tried immediately to open his eyes. His eyelids looked as if they were glued together. Eventually he forced them open while I was still looking at him at close range. When his eyes were wide open, I asked him if he had been asleep. 'No,' he said, happily.

As I drove home in my car, I thought nobody would believe me. I was still puzzled about what exactly had happened.

The answer came two months later.

An Indian gentleman came for an appointment for the first time. As always I asked what he did for living in order to get a better understanding of his physical condition. He told me that he was a hypnotist working on stage in Kenya. I then told him the story about Mr. G.

The Indian gentleman explained to me how I had conditioned Mr. G. slowly into a hypnotic trance till in the end he could not resist my instructions any longer and he had fallen asleep. He also pointed out that by mentioning my dream I had put Mr. G. straight into a dream state, the deepest level in hypnosis you can reach. Apparently I had made a mistake by asking Mr. G. to wiggle the toes on his bad foot. If I had said left foot he probably would have done it, though it was paralysed.

I later found with other stroke patients how easy they were to hypnotise. There was hardly any resistance. They responded extremely well to hypnotic suggestions, often improving physically as well. It meant that new or different nerve pathways were being used by the patient, which is something that I believe should be researched further by the medical profession.

10 In At The Deep End

After the hypnotic experience with Mr. G., I came to the conclusion that I now needed to study about what I now realised I had the skill to do, hypnotise people!

I had no idea how to go about it so decided to look for adverts in a Health Magazine. Almost immediately I found an advert, 'Last person wanted for new hypnotherapy class.' I didn't need any further encouragement.

We had to work in pairs and it seemed straight away as if it was meant for me. I joined a small school of Hypno- and Psycho- Therapy in 1988 and passed the diploma course after two years.

At this point my colleague's patient was looking for a hypnotherapist. Apparently Mrs. K. had held a phobia for many years. She had been to many therapists without success. I was not particularly confident that I could help her when so many others, all long established hypnotherapists, could not affect a cure.

Mrs. K. suffered from a feeling of jerking and falling forward when at work, sitting in a meeting or when closing her eyes saying a prayer. This complaint had begun after the birth of her first child, twelve years ago.

Neither x-rays, examinations by a nose, throat and ear specialist nor homeopathy could find the cause or even just make her feel better. Mrs. K. was now quite desperate as this problem severely disrupted her life. She had rapidly lost her confidence – especially when coping with her executive-type position at work. When she gave interviews she was terribly nervous that she would fall off her chair. This anxiety overcame her also in public places.

During a deep tissue massage (which can sometimes be quite painful) Mrs. K and I got to know each other. I sensed how much more at ease she was with me as I tuned in with her. The more she felt comfortable with me, the better I found I could work with her. She gave me all necessary details about her past, her family life and her medication.

After the massage I let her get dressed and asked her to lie on my hypnosis couch. I covered her up with a blanket. It made her feel safe. Most people prefer that. Then I explained how hypnosis works and what it is.

There are four stages of hypnosis: stage one is a kind of self-hypnosis, such as day dreaming. We all do it naturally; when we drive from A to B and go on automatic pilot, that is a kind of self-hypnosis as is meditation and, probably, prayer.

In the second stage the client feels perhaps a sense of pins and needles in their limbs, or they become heavy in the body. The person can still hear all the noises that are going on around them and is still aware of the hypnotherapist talking to them.

I usually explain before the session that it is more productive not to raise objections to things I mention during hypnosis. Clients disagreeing mentally or going in for talking on their own account can make them use their rational thought and censorship and they can sometimes bring themselves back out of hypnosis that way. It is particularly relevant during a first session.

Stage Three of hypnosis is when the clients start to 'lose me' on and off during the hypnotic session. This often means that they are making journeys into stage four, the deepest stage, when they become in a dream- like state. When that happens I usually talk more loudly and tell them not to lose me at any time. Otherwise they may argue that they were asleep and had had to pay for that because they didn't remember much of what was been going on.

I also explained to Mrs. K. that hypnosis is an altered state of awareness. We use it often when we, rhythmically stroke a baby or a dog. The baby or dog tends to fall instantly into a deep hypnotic sleep. That is how natural and normal the hypnotic state actually is.

In our everyday life we use the left hemisphere of our brain for our rational thought processes. If we are left-handed it will be the right side of the brain. This rational thinking side we use mainly in work conditions or stress situations. It is governed by beta brainwaves, which run at 14 – 21 brain cycles per second; anything higher indicates a stress, a headache or possibly the onset of a migraine.

Alfa brainwaves run at 7 to 14 brain cycles per second and are slower. We might normally use them just before we go to sleep, as this is the time when we are mentally slowing down. The same applies to meditation. Theta brain waves are even slower, and can run at 4 - 7 and 1 – 4 cycles per second. These indicate deep sleep or even unconsciousness. We do not need to access them in hypnosis.

The first hypnotic session always follows my massage. It tends to take away physical and mental blocks so the patient can drift easily into a relaxed and happy frame of mind, into what I call a healing hypnosis. The client will wake up refreshed, confident and happy.

Mrs. K. told me that she slept extremely well after the session for a few nights. She was still suffering from the strange jerking but was looking forward to the next meeting.

During this session I regressed her to a situation in the past, which was relevant to the jerks. Almost instantly she started to fidget and almost woke herself up. I told her it was not important and took her in her mind to a beautiful garden. Here I asked her to connect with the energy of the grass under the soles of her bare feet; to breathe in the peace in the garden and harmony around her, to look at the varied colours of the different flowers, to listen to the songs of the birds and to feel the warmth and power of the sun, thus making her feel extremely strong, healthy and calm, and raising her self-esteem.

I asked her to imagine the sun becoming the white light in the universe and to tune in with the unconditional love it stands for, with its inbuilt happiness and aura of absolute success. Anything she wanted to master she could now achieve, provided it enhanced her in body, mind and spirit which automatically enhances all mankind, as we are all connected along what I like to call the love vibration.

The next step was to put her into a situation in which she normally would start to jerk. I put her mentally into a board meeting. As soon as I mentioned the meeting, I also pointed out the total strength and energy she now had, emphasising that she was in complete control of the situation at all times. The light and love that was now engulfing her would always put her on the winning side, her side. 'You are a winner!' I told her.

When she woke up she seemed uplifted yet apprehensive at the same time. She realised that the jerking had momentarily disappeared. She asked me point blank, 'What if it comes back?'

I did not know what to say, as none of my textbooks had raised that question. She immediately picked up on my hesitation and indecisive attitude. Instantly she started jerking again. I was devastated.

Convinced that I needed more study into psychology, I started a degree course at Birkbeck College, London University and eventually gained an honours degree.

Many years later a patient asked me that same question again, 'What if it comes back?'

This time I answered without hesitation, 'No problem! We can always reinforce the treatment with another hypnotic session, if that is necessary.'

Needless to say, it was not.

This shows how an insecure person believes completely in their therapist. They then have to be gently taught to stand on their own two feet and to believe in themselves.

I have also found, whenever you change something from a long-standing negative to a positive one, you take the body out of its long-standing negative balance, as the body / mind compensates, so life can go on. It can often remain unstable until the positive balance establishes itself along with the feeling of complete control once again.

11 Not Everybody Wants To Get Better

Mr. and Mrs S. were a quite well off couple. He had been a successful builder but had now retired. Mrs. S. then suffered a sudden stroke. It seemed so severe that her husband was now forced to do everything for her: light her cigarettes, help her to eat all her meals, turn her around in bed and so on. Needless to say he became very weary of it all, and in his desperation he engaged a physiotherapist and me, then a masseuse.

Time went by. We were all working very hard with Mrs S. to achieve an improvement. She did not seem to respond to treatment at all, but seemed in herself quite happy.

One day, after I had massaged her, I introduced some passive movements for her affected arm, which was limp. I supported the arm and gently lifted it upwards to help the circulation and take the arm through its range of movement.

As I lifted the arm slowly up and down with concentration, Mrs. S. was looking out of the window. She seemed to be paying no attention to our exercise at all and said suddenly, 'Is it raining outside?' This show of total apathy and the pressure from her husband, wanting to know why she wasn't getting any better, made me suddenly very cross. In a sharp tone I commanded her to concentrate on her arm and try to lift it. To my amazement, and hers, I felt her arm, which I had been supporting, become lighter. Then she lifted it without my help.

She was in tears. She genuinely had not known that she was still able to do that. At the same time she begged me not to tell her husband, as he would make her do it all the time.

I realised then that all her married life Mr. S. had been out working and had had little time for her. Now she had him pinned down by being helpless. She had gained what she had always wanted: her husband's total attention!

As Mr. S. complained again about her not advancing in any way, I could not help saying to myself, 'Sometimes people just don't want to get better.'

12 Sometimes People Want To Get Better Consciously But Not Unconsciously

A colleague told me this story about something that had happened to him. As I am on the subject of the mind, I feel it is particularly relevant to mention it.

A friend had recommended a lady who was suffering with multiple sclerosis. This lady arrived in a wheelchair. She wanted physical therapy to help her to walk again.

After some weeks of treatment she was making remarkable progress. The therapist, who was also a cranial therapist, felt that there were some emotional blocks hampering further recovery.

Cranial sacral therapy is extremely gentle. Just a touch of the fingertips is all that is necessary. The therapist looks for the cranial rhythm. There is no force at all. It was suggested to this lady that she try this therapy, and she agreed.

Just one session made her feel worse. She stopped any further treatment. She did not respond to any other treatments, including acupuncture, either. The lady who had brought her in explained that she had had a fall later and broken her femur. She was in hospital for weeks and began to get worse daily. Before she died, she confided in her friend that she and her husband had had a child. He had been born severely retarded and had been in a home for many years. Her husband had died many years before she had developed multiple sclerosis. Their child had been born two years after they had married and from that point on her husband had ruled against her having another child.

She had silently suffered for many years.

Her conscious mind seemed to have allowed her physical improvement, but the unconscious mind was dealing with deeper issues. She was unconsciously not prepared to open those wounds again. She probably opted for another way out: to die instead.

13 It Can Be Fatal Not To Keep A Promise To Yourself

Mr. B. had been smoking cigars for many years. About a year ago his elderly mother had died. He was very close to her and it had hit him hard. In addition to this he had recently been diagnosed with cancer in one lung.

When he came to see me he had just finished a few weeks of radium therapy. He looked thin and weak from his sickness. His wife had suggested hypnotherapy to which he had in desperation agreed.

I felt that Mr. B. would benefit from a healing hypnosis. After I induced him, sending him deeper into a hypnotic state, I directed him mentally to a place of his choice, which he would enjoy. Before such sessions I invariably ask my clients about their favourite places; for instance a beach, a garden, a mountain or even a hot air balloon.

Mr. B. chose a garden, somewhere he had never actually been to before. He therefore had no real memories in this garden that he could relate to. I let him feel the energy of growing grass, made him aware of the colours of different flowers, asked him to notice their fragrances, to connect with the blue sky and to listen to the birds singing. It is important in such moments to engage all five senses. The more real it feels, the better it works. Then I asked him to place himself under a gentle fountain, washing away all the negative emotions that might be trapped in the aura that is the energy field that surrounds us all.

I suggested that the water of this special fountain ran not only externally but also internally through his body. At the same time I named all the areas and organs in his body which the water of the magic fountain cleanses, renews and re-energises, especially those which were in need of 're-balancing'.

I then asked Mr. B. in his imagination to lie on the grass relaxed; to look into the deep blue sky, breathing the blue, healing colour into his head, into all the areas of the left and right hemisphere of his brain, saturating each brain cell. The healing vibration of the blue colour would then penetrate the conscious mind with its rational thinking and its censorship, particularly advancing into the area where thoughts arise. Under hypnosis you will always know exactly where that is. I asked him to replace any negative thoughts with happy, uplifting and constructive ones. Pointing out that actions would follow the thoughts, I suggested that from now, he would be only interested in thinking and doing those things which would enrich him in body, mind and spirit.

It is my belief that we are a spirit with a body. The conscious mind contains everything from birth until now. Half of it is forgotten and appears in the pre-conscious mind, according to Jung. The rarely understood unconscious mind can be seen as the main part of the brain. It contains all knowledge about us, however far-reaching our past is. The unconscious mind also contains our dream department, an area that deals with creativity, with such as things we enjoy seeing or doing, as they relax us.

Returning to Mr. B. who was still deeply hypnotised and lying on the grass of his beautiful garden, I suggested focusing onto the sun in the sky, drawing the warmth of the sunshine into his skin, and making him feel save and secure, yet totally in control of the situation at all times.

I told him he was now connecting with the sun in the sky in his imagination, which would become the golden white light in his universe. This light stands for unconditional love. The Light and the Love will always become the focal point of all positive changes in our lives. Mr. B. wanted to make changes. He wanted to stop smoking.

As he welcomed this unconditional love and light into his body, mind and spirit, I wanted to help him understand that it signified total success, total forgiveness, total truth and could be totally trusted. All the changes Mr. B. wanted to make, it wouldn't matter how many, he could consider them granted, provided they enhanced him in body, mind and spirit, automatically involving all mankind, as we are all connected. It is important that negative wishes are not granted as they can hamper spiritual development, and make people physically ill.

I told Mr. B. to breathe in and absorb the white light which was healing, harmonising and balancing all areas, particularly the lung area. The more you repeat suggestions under hypnosis the better they will work. I asked him to become aware of how cleansed the alveoli in his lungs are and how he could now breathe in much more deeply. I asked him to saturate every cell of his body with this unconditional love, making him feel fit, strong and healthy.

I also explained how his body, and in particular his lungs, was willing to accept a promise he was about to make to himself: 'I know that my lungs will re-generate to total health and stay that way, provided I never smoke again from now on... That is the deal!'

With this strong affirmation, he woke up from his hypnotic state a very positive and happy person. Within a few weeks he looked so well. He put on weight again. He told everybody in his local pub about what had happened to him. He recommended me to the landlord's wife, who was suffering from widespread cancer. She was eventually sent to my clinic by her husband. Unfortunately, she did not want to be in my clinic to be treated. Needless to say, after the first treatment she did not make another appointment. It is impossible and even pointless to treat patients against their will. I will often ask such patients, 'Do you want to be here in my clinic or are you just doing somebody a favour?'

Mr. B. looked so well. He worked again but I only saw him occasionally.

One day many years later I learned from a friend of his that he had started smoking again. I reminded him of his promise and warned him what a very dangerous thing it is to lie to yourself in such situations.

Anything could happen.

14 Wise Words

Watch your thoughts, they become words.

Watch your words, they become actions.

Watch your actions, they become habits.

Watch your habits, they become character.

Watch your character, it becomes your destiny.

Frank Outlaw

15 Don't Ask What A Disease A Person Has, But What Person Has A Disease?

Mr. F. received a weekly massage from me for his stiffened back. In the past, over a length of time, he had suffered three different spinal fusions, in the lower back, in the middle part and the vertebrae of the neck. When he was turning from one side to the other, I could not fail to notice the rigidity of the whole spine.

During various treatments we would invariably chat. Mr. F. was always very polite. He would discuss any subject but himself. If I asked him a personal question, everything was 'always fine.' He never showed his feelings and emotions.

During one particular session, using GAI (Guided Affected Imagery) everything was once more 'always fine'. I asked him to visualise a meadow he had never actually seen before and describe just what came into his mind. He told me that it was 'nice'. The stream I asked him to imagine was 'clear'. The house I asked him to picture was 'perfect'. Then I suggested he venture upstairs into the house.

I asked how many rooms there were upstairs. 'Three,' he answered. He entered two rooms easily. By his descriptions, these two rooms were boring and plain. Then I told him to enter room number three. He started getting frustrated and impatient and protested that he couldn't go in. He hesitated and then said the door had been wallpapered over. I laughed, 'No problem.' Trading off the fact that he had told me the room had windows, I countered that one of them was open and there was a ladder in the garden which he should climb, look through the window and report to me what was in the room. Without much enthusiasm he commented that the room had lovely wallpaper and was . . . empty!

The whole exercise upset him. My probing made him feel quite uncomfortable. With relief he had found the room was empty.

His wife told me later that Mr. F.'s parents were also strange. Even when he was a child he would never really talk to them about anything he regarded as personal. Nobody in the family showed their feelings. They had never discussed anything unpleasant. Problems just did not exist as far as they were concerned.

Mrs. F., his wife, was quite an outspoken lady. She believed in bringing things out into the open. If something was bothering her about their relationship she would tell him. As soon as she started arguing about a problem, Mr. F. would go out. Two hours later he would re-appear and make out as if nothing had happened. It drove his wife to despair.

Carl Rogers in his Seven Stages Hypothesis from 'Fixity to Flowingness' traces this progression.

I took Mrs. F. through the four stages, and this shed light on her husband's outlook: there is never any problem, even if there is a big one that needs addressing.

Mr. F. was still physically rigid in his spine, due to many spinal fusions, and he was also mentally rigid in his way of thinking, his outlook and his conversation. Emotions are suppressed and ignored. It raises the question: Has the rigid outlook affected his body or vice versa?

In stage two of Carl Rogers' hypothesis the patient will acknowledge that there is a problem, but it is generally seen as entirely somebody else's fault.

In stage three, there will be a problem which is mainly somebody else's fault, but a small part might be related to oneself.

In stage four the patient begins to accept 'There is a problem. What can 'I' do about it? How can 'I' change it?'

Mrs. F. was as far as I could see on stage four in terms of dealing with disagreements in their marriage. Mr. F., in comparison, was on stage one. He ignored any problems.

As I explained these stages to her, I could sense her understanding the whole situation far better. I explained that with much caring, kindness and unconditional love, disputes could be conquered slowly. Mr. F. needed to be able to trust his wife totally. Blame, arguments, anger and shouting would only close him down further.

Married couples are often on different stages of understanding that this model provides. These are the main reasons for disputes. How many marriages could be saved by learning to understand each other and by making allowances for the different stages of development we are experiencing?

16 From The Fixed To The Flowing

Carl Rogers has hypothesised that individuals are, at any given time in their lives, in one or more of the seven processes by which they move from

from the fixed to the flowing

Stage One is characterised by the following: communication is only about external things and not about the self

- Personal feelings and meanings are neither recognised nor owned.
- Elements of the personality are rigidly constructed.
- Close relationships are construed as dangerous.
- Intimate communication is construed as dangerous.
- Problems are not recognised.
- There is no desire to change.
- There is a blockage of internal communication.
- The client perceives experiences to be like those of the past and then reacts to the past with all its attendant feelings.

Stage Two is characterised by the following:

- Problems are perceived as external to the self.
- Expression begins to flow in regard to non-self topics.
- There is no sense of personal responsibility in problems.
- Exhibited feelings are not recognised or 'owned'.
- Fixed elements of the personality are thought of as unbending facts.
- Personal feelings are very limited and global.

Stage Three is characterised by the following:

- A freer flow of expression about the self.
- Some expression about self-relating experiences.
- Expression about the self as existing in others.
- Expression of feelings and meanings not now present.
- Feelings are usually negative with little acceptance of them.
- Experience is described as the past, remote from the self.
- Personal feelings are more in focus and less global.
- Personal choices are often seen as ineffective.

Stage Four is characterised by the following:
- Feelings of the past, not recognised as being in the present, are described more intensely.
- Occasionally feelings are expressed in terms of the present.
- There is a fear and distrust of experiencing feelings in the present as they occur.
- There is an acceptance of feelings exhibited on small scale.
- Experience is less remote and bound by the past.
- The patient begins to question the validity of rigid elements of the personality as they become apparent.
- There are feelings of self-responsibility in problems.
- Small risks are now taken in close relationships.

Stage Five is characterised by the following:
- Feelings are expressed as in the present.
- Feelings are very close to being fully experienced, despite occasional fear and distrust.
- There is surprise expressed at experiencing the feelings.
- There is an increasing desire to be the 'real me.'
- Experiencing feelings is no longer a remote process.
- There is a critical examination of newly discovered aspects of the personality.
- There is an increasing acceptance of self-responsibility.
- There is a reduction of internal blockage of communication.

Stage Six is characterised by the following:
- An inhibited feeling is now experienced with immediacy.
- Feelings now flow to their full extent.
- All present feelings are directly experienced.
- Feelings are not denied, feared, nor fought against, but accepted.
- The self is the feeling.
- There is physiological freedom to accompany the feelings.
- There is freedom from the constraints of the rigid elements of the personality.
- The client is now 'living the problem'; it is no longer an object.

Stage Seven is characterised by the following:

- New feelings are experienced with immediacy, both in the therapeutic relationship and outside.
- There is an increasing trust in the acceptance of feelings.
- The present experiences are not interpreted as the past.
- The self is less frequently a perceived object.
- Internal communication is now clear.
- An effective choice of new ways of being is experienced.

17 Nothing Ever Happens Accidentally

Both, my husband and I were fully booked in our clinic for the whole week.

My husband suddenly felt unwell and I had to cancel his patients for that day. I managed to reach everybody by telephone but for one man, Mr K., who was due to come over at 6pm. It was lucky that his and my appointment with another patient only slightly overlapped. For a short while I put Mr. K. on our electro magnetic machine for his back pain.

When I took him off the machine and he stood in front of me I noticed that he was trembling badly in his left arm and shoulder. He also stuttered as he talked to me. He explained that it had all started six months earlier and that he had been diagnosed with Parkinson's syndrome. They were uncertain whether he had the fully developed form of the disease.

I enquired about what had happened in his life in the last two years. He replied that his eighty-five year old mother had died one year before his shaking started. He also told me that he missed her very much.

I wondered why he had made himself ill over it as she had reached a good age.

Somehow I wanted to make him feel better, mentally. I explained a way he might look at his situation. If we were a spirit with a body and could see the mind as a go between, the conscious mind would be more connected with the body and everyday life, with the unconscious mind more connected with the soul and the universe. In this situation, our spirit, our life force, could not die. I told him to imagine his mother was alive as a spirit and he was connected through the love they had for each other, so she could feel what he felt. This would mean that he was fretting for her so much that he had actually made himself ill. She would be able to pick that up.

I then treated Mr. K's back on my plinth. I had a strong feeling that I needed to apply some healing to his still shaking arm and shoulder. Mr. K. agreed to the healing and as I gently put my hands onto the area, his shaking increased dramatically. I sensed that he was worried about it getting worse and re-assured him, 'If it gets worse, it also gets better!' At the same time I told myself that it wouldn't do to say just that to him.

After two minutes the shaking lessened. He got up and said without stuttering, 'It's gone!'

'For now,' I answered. 'The cause is still there somewhere.'

'Do you want to know how my mother died?' he asked. I reassured him that he didn't have to tell me. 'But I want to tell you,' he insisted. 'My mother and I had an argument and she drowned herself in the Thames.'

It began to make sense. I explained, 'You are punishing yourself and are trying to substitute Parkinson's syndrome for your guilt feelings.

'You know your mother would not like that. She would want to tell you that it was an accident. She knows you love her very much. If you didn't love her, you would not have made yourself ill over it.'

One lady I knew, who had originally come to me as a patient, was Mrs M., an eighty year old medium. She was a fascinating woman and I learned a great deal from her. I used to pick her up from her son's house by car as she had no transport.

This particular evening, after Mr. K. had left our clinic, I fetched the old lady to take her home. Over a cup of tea I told her the story of the man and his mother. After listening for a few minutes she announced, 'There are some anemones falling on your lap.' And then, when I gave her a quizzical look, she said, "Does that mean anything to you?

'No, not really,' I answered in disbelief. I certainly did not see anything.

After a short hesitation, she explained, 'They're from that man's mother to say thank you for the rescue work you have done for them both.'

I found myself becoming embarrassed, thinking she did not need to make all that up.

The following week Mr. K. turned up for his next appointment. I wondered whether to tell him what the old lady had said and then I just told him anyway, but it did not make any sense to him at all. I immediately regretted mentioning it.

At his appointment one week later, very excited, he informed me that his wife had told him anemones were his mother's favourite flowers.

18 Connecting Physical Therapy With Mental Therapy

Mrs. A. was extremely depressed when she rang me. I treated her the same day, as she was feeling suicidal.

During my usual deep tissue massage she explained her background. She was an only child. Her parents were well to do. They were often out of the country when Mrs. A. was a little girl. Therefore she had attended boarding school from a young age.

It was expected of her that she would do well in everything she studied. Mrs. A. had been a very obedient child. She became head girl at school and generally complied with everything her parents, in particular her mother, instructed her to do.

She married somebody from a higher profession. They had two children and lived in a very fashionable part of town, next to a well-known artist. All seemed well, although Mrs. A. was somewhat overweight, even as a child.

When Mrs. A. mentioned to her mother that she wanted to study a particular subject at university, her mother immediately opposed her idea as unsuitable and suggested another subject instead.

Mrs. A. was extremely disturbed about the new suggestion. It seemed to be the last straw, too demanding of obedience even for her.

Verbally she rebelled on my couch. She was ready not to surrender to her mother's wishes anymore. One could detect anger, frustration and near hatred in her voice and expressions. At the same time she was also devastated about her mother's selfishness. I could detect a feeling of guilt. Mrs. A. wanted to find the courage to stay with her principles. She begged me to make her feel better and asked for a session of hypnosis as well as the massage.

Until the day Mrs. A. arrived, I had always separated any physical treatments I was administering from mental treatments. I believed to combine the two would be too much for anyone. At the same time I found that the first hypnotic session for any patient never worked nearly as well as the second or subsequent ones. People wanted consciously to be hypnotised, because that was in simple terms what they had come there for. Unconsciously it was a different matter. Most of the time they behaved nervously at the first session, afraid of various imagined aspects of hypnosis. They were also often not deeply relaxed. Nevertheless, after the first treatment they usually could not wait for the next one.

Deep tissue massage, especially treatment of trigger points is painful, but relaxes the person physically and mentally. Trigger points are found in tight muscles, especially between the shoulder blades and the spine. They feel to the therapists often like tiny stones or a mesh of tiny muscle areas. They are also often found to contain among waste products various stored negative emotions from the past. When one presses these points there is often great pain reported, like a knife, needle or burning, which radiates deeply, either up, down or sideways.

When these trigger points are released, people often open up about their innermost secrets, frequently talking about unhappy times in their lives. In other words, released trigger points will help facilitate successful mental treatment such as hypnotherapy.

I asked Mrs. A. to come back another day for her hypnotherapy appointment. She was adamant that I could not send her home still feeling awful and insisted on having a hypnotherapy session. I reluctantly proposed a short session, just half an hour, to which she agreed.

The hypnosis went well due to the massage beforehand. Using positive affirmations, suggesting uplifting thoughts, actions and ideas, she soon looked contented. The blue sky with the healing colour indigo was used to balance and harmonise her way of thinking along with the sunshine, its golden white light standing for unconditional love and enlightenment. I emphasised total confidence in her, a greater self-esteem and happiness from deep within, most importantly to retrieve her sense of humour again, and rebuild it.

After the session she went from rock bottom to sky high. She went home happy.

That same evening she telephoned me and said, 'We are having a party tonight and I am feeling marvellous!'

I immediately calmed her down, 'It won't last the way it is. I just wanted to show you how happy one can feel, as you had forgotten that. You will go down again but not to rock bottom as it was to start with. Gradually with each session you will feel better. That way it will be more lasting.'

Her next appointment was for the Monday. Sunday evening she phoned me again and said apologetically, 'I can't come anymore! I told everybody at my church how well and happy I am feeling. They said that hypnosis is evil!'

What a shame.

Mrs. A. was still conforming to what others told her.

19 What We Eat And Drink, How We Breathe, And Think, Is What We Are!

The most effective way of learning is always the hardest way.

As I was born during the end of the Second World War, food was hard to come by. My family were evacuated into a tiny village in Germany and lived in just one room. It was the belief in those days that sugar, and in particular glucose, gave you energy. My parents told me later that they had put glucose into my milk right from the start. As you will gather, I soon became a sugar junkie.

Up to the age of fourteen I was one of the best pupils in class, and just before my fifteenth birthday I got into the habit of buying a bar of chocolate daily with my pocket money. Within six months my concentration went completely. When the teacher asked me to read a passage out of a book and to talk about it, I could not retain the contents. In fact it seemed as if they had never reached my brain. I was always tired, although I went to bed early. All I was ever looking forward to was the bar of chocolate!

During my time at college and my later time working in an office, I was always exhausted. Getting through the day proved to be torture. I forgot everything my boss asked me to do. I had blank spells. When I was typing I sometimes left half a sentence out. I could not be bothered to read through reports I had to write for my boss. I was just so tired. My body seemed to weigh a ton. The only way I could go out with my friends in the evening was by drinking alcohol. It seemed to pick me up.

The next morning I paid for it. I felt worse than ever.

Although I seemed to be forever sleepy throughout the day, I could not sleep deeply at night. Eventually I saw my GP. The doctor explained that I had hypoglycemia, which meant that my blood sugar was too low. He suggested eating more frequently.

As I thought about the problem, I came to the conclusion that if the blood sugar were too low, I would need to eat food with lots of sugar to increase it. I soon introduced lots of fruit into my diet. I ate a pound of bananas in one go. Another time I consumed a monstrous bunch of grapes, and then some more. Needless to say, I felt desperately weak, because of the intake of fructose. When people talked to me I would go through the motions of answering but it felt in reality as if I was talking to them all through a glass window. I couldn't connect properly with people. It was all a bit of a fog.

I passed my examinations with great difficulty and with not particularly impressive grades.

Then, at 21, I came to England, continuing my sugar-filled diet to which I added English biscuits, ice cream and cake. Throughout my early life I had had a trim figure, but in no time I put on 20 pounds. My new boyfriend, now my husband, bought me a new skirt as nothing fitted me anymore.

At that time I was an au pair, also studying English at college every day. I was so exhausted physically and mentally I was forgetting everything. I dragged myself through the day. When the 75 year old ironing lady came to do her work, singing to herself and looking fit and healthy, I thought, why am I so tired? I came to the conclusion that I'd never reach fifty.

I married my husband at the age of 24. A year later I was pregnant with our first child. I decided that he should be made of good stuff, so I ate only healthy food. No sweets, some fruit, but not in excess, a lot of greens and salads and protein.

After the first three months of morning sickness, I felt fantastic. My body was strong, my mind was clear, and I could suddenly remember things. In the past I had lost all my confidence because I had become unreliable and also very clumsy. At the same time I knew that I was not stupid. The new diet during my pregnancy made me enthusiastic, positive and self-assured. My self-esteem rose to a new high.

I came to the conclusion that pregnancy suited me. At the same time I realised that I could not have one child after another just to feel good.

After my son was born I slowly slipped back into my old eating habits. In my mid-thirties I found myself as useless as before. To sum up, on my weekly shop I would start on a bar of chocolate in the supermarket and later, at the till, all I would have to show the check-out girl was the empty wrapper.

After we moved into our latest house, I had just passed my basic massage course. This particular evening I had just finished work. Exhausted, as usual, I plunged into a chair in my waiting room. At random I picked up a magazine. My attention was drawn to an article about a famous actress. I read that she had been suffering from hypoglycemia. With interest I read that she had gone through exactly the same experiences I had been tormented by. She began to forget her lines when she was on stage and had to have a bite of a mars bar so she could remember the rest.

The magazine article gave the scientific explanation. Hypoglycemia (low blood sugar) increases with the intake of any sugars such as glucose, sucrose and fructose. Each time a person consumes these items in excess or too quickly, the pancreas increases its production of insulin to lower blood sugar. The pancreas can overcompensate, just in case there is a further amount of sugar to follow which could raise the blood sugar level through the roof. Too much sugar in the blood is just as dangerous as too little. In severe cases it can lead to a diabetic coma and even death.

Sugar is a fast-burning carbohydrate. You could compare it to a fire which is fed with just balls of newspaper. There would be a short big flame. No heat would radiate from it, but there would still be a certain amount of ash left behind.

Sugar does the same to a person: there is a high burst of energy until the pancreas overcompensates and reduces the blood sugar level to less than it was before. A considerable amount of acid is left behind. Generally speaking sugar makes acid and salads, as well as green vegetables, make alkaline in the body.

It is important that we eat slow-burning carbohydrates. There are two kinds: starchy carbohydrates such as potatoes, bread, pasta and rice, and fibrous carbohydrates such as leafy greens found in salads and green vegetables.

Again let's look at the analogy with the fire. Imagine you put wood on a fire. It will give you a considerable amount of warmth but only for a specific length of time. This time the span would be equivalent to the time span of the energy you would receive when you eat slow-burning carbohydrates.

Imagine now that there is a fire, which you feed with coal. It will take a certain amount of time to burn through and then for another length of time it will continue burning until eventually it will require more coal, or the fire will go out.

This could be compared with eating proteins such as those found in fish, meat, cheese and eggs. Protein gives us energy that lasts for a much longer time than carbohydrates do.

Who should eat more carbohydrates, and who should eat more protein?

I found that people who tend to be overweight have generally a slower metabolism than thinner people who have a generally faster one. People with a faster metabolism can eat more carbohydrates whereas those with a slower metabolism tend to gain weight more easily. For them, protein might be more advisable in combination with greens.

I am not a dietitian, nor am I a nutritionist. These are only my observations. Once I began to follow these guidelines, I improved my strength, mental brain power and sleep patterns.

Which leads me to another issue I often find in my patients. Just why do so many people suffer from insomnia? To answer that, we need to look at their sleep pattern. Some people cannot fall asleep easily. However, when they eventually do, they will sleep all night. These people might be suffering from the stress and tension of the day, or be trying to sleep on an empty stomach.

There is another category of person who falls asleep easily but wakes up after just a few hours. They then cannot fall asleep again. These people might be suffering from a combination of stress and hypoglycemia. If they get up when they wake up and eat a sandwich and have a hot drink, they would probably sleep soundly for the rest of the night.

So why do they become hypoglycemic during the night?

We have to take a closer look at their diet, especially what they eat or drink last thing at night. Often people have their last big meal early in the evening. About three to four hours later they go to bed. It is too long for this kind of diet to last through the night as the sugar level will slowly decrease over the ensuing hours. When it becomes too low for comfort, the person will wake up. It is an inbuilt survival system.

If people eat dinner early in the evening, they may often snack before they go to bed. Often it will be chocolate, or a glass of wine or even hot sweet drinks. Overnight these will decrease the blood sugar level because the pancreas may over-supply insulin. Years of continuous stimulation and overuse of the pancreas can lead to the pancreas insufficiency known more familiarly as diabetes.

Alcohol is made of sugar, as are sweet soft drinks. If they do not contain sugar, such as diet-sweet soft drinks, they often contain harmful chemicals which are only added to enhance colour, smell or taste.

Fruit juices, which contain no sugar, are full of concentrated fructose. The body translates such an input into eating a few spoonfuls of sweet stuff. Dried fruit contains a large amount of concentrated fructose. If you are already suffering from too much sugar intake, leave it alone. There are many hidden sugars in sauces, processed foods, tinned foods and even ham. I would always advise reading the shop labels that will give you the contents of any food. The closer to the top of the list sugar is as an ingredient, the higher the percentage of the foodstuff, and the more likely it is to do you harm.

20 Candida (Yeast Overgrowth)

Ms S. told me that she worked in a hospital research department and was due for her Masters degree examination (MSc) in three weeks time.

She was not worried about the examination, as she knew her subject well. She was more concerned about her inability to retain what she was learning. 'Everything is in a fog, I can't think straight!' she told me. 'My short-term memory seems non-existent.'

Looking at her lifestyle, especially her diet, I soon realised that she had a sugar problem. As there was never enough time for proper meals, she snacked, particularly on chocolates, at various times during the day. Sweet soft drinks were used as her daily fluid intake.

I realised that she needed to change her diet and eliminate the sugary items as soon as possible. I was also aware that a sudden change of diet, and thereby a starving of the addiction, would take her on a downhill journey for at least a few weeks. In the cold turkey part of this treatment, the cravings would set in with a vengeance. It would not have been the right time to introduce a total correction of her diet just before the examination.

In the end I decided to suggest she kept on eating her chocolates for the time being. I urged her to introduce protein such as fish, chicken, and slow-burning carbohydrates, such as potatoes, rice and greens as they would help stabilise the sugar levels in the blood for the time being.

In the long run her lifestyle needed improving: Enough sleep, a small regular meal, every two to three hours. In the morning she should have porridge and maybe mid-morning have some natural almonds if she was not allergic to them. At lunch-time I would recommend fish or chicken with a salad, in the afternoon maybe a sandwich or some more almonds and then later her evening meal, but no dessert.

The problem time, from dinner until bedtime, needed to be filled with sensible snacks. Most people have a glass of wine, with some biscuits or crisps. Instead I suggested perhaps a little more protein if she was still hungry. If not, maybe a small bowl of porridge, which would help the body keep the blood sugar at a certain level throughout the night. It could also improve her sleep pattern greatly.

With hypnosis I reinforced the diet in her mind. With ego-boosting techniques I reassured her that she would retrieve all she had ever learned about the subject she was studying as soon as she read the examination questions.

The lady was pleased with her newly-found relaxed state and self-assurance. She wanted to return after the examination to further develop her new life style.

21 Can Too Much Sugar Really Be The Reason For Food Allergies?

Mrs. B. suffered from aches and pains particularly in her legs and also partly in her hands, shoulders and neck. She had had medication in the past, which did not seem to have helped. Eventually it was explained to her 'It is all in your mind. There is nothing physically wrong with you.'

She saw a practitioner privately in Harley Street. He took into consideration her daily intake of food and suggested that she take no sugar in any form.

Fresh fruit and honey was encouraged.

Mrs. B. started to feel much better, up to a point. 'After a few weeks it seemed to stay at a certain level of improvement and would not improve any further,' she complained, when she saw me.

I suggested, 'Try to eliminate fruit and honey as well for at least a week,' hinting that she could feel much worse or a good deal better. Any reaction would be an encouraging sign. If she felt exactly the same, sugar was not her problem - unless she had cheated.

When someone continues having no sugar, fructose or glucose in any form, they may reach a crisis point. Even their way of thinking and reasoning might be affected. They might tell themselves one sweet or a piece of fruit won't hurt, but all sugar does is prepare you for more sugar.

Mrs. B. was eager to try the new diet I'd suggested. Instead of sugar, more vegetables and salads plus protein were introduced. Hypnosis was a helpful reinforcement to stay with her diet. Within two weeks she had lost seven pounds, and was delighted. The pain in her limbs began to fade as she passed weeks three and four. Mrs. B. began to felt brighter and continued to improve. She stayed with her weekly deep tissue massage and was soon her old happy self again.

Then, suddenly, she announced that she and her husband were moving house. Her stress levels changed dramatically. Unfortunately her diet did as well. Convenience foods were consumed more frequently. Mrs. B. explained to me that she intended to return to her strictly no sugar diet as soon as possible. I warned her that the second time around it would be much more difficult to stay with it.

A few months later a heavier Mrs. B. arrived, in great pain again. She told me she felt far worse than before. She still enjoyed the massages but now went to a different practitioner for allergy testing. It was discovered that she was not allergic to sugar, but to dairy products and to gluten. The result was that she continued with her sugar intake and left out the foods she knew she was allergic to.

After a few weeks she became far worse. The practitioner sent her to a diet specialist who gave her steroids for her condition. She ballooned and her illness increased dramatically. She ended up in hospital unable to move without pain.

My theory is that if sugar is your problem, then avoid it. If you do not avoid it – the acid in your body will increase. Generally, sugar makes acid and vegetables, including salads, make alkaline in the body. With food allergies, sugar seems to be the cause. If you refrain only from the foods you are allergic to and keep sugar in your diet, it will result in more and different allergies.

My recommendation would be to take sugar and the foods you are allergic or addicted to, out of your diet. This way you probably will improve your immune system considerably. In any case, even if you do not have a sugar problem, it will certainly enhance your health. Unfortunately there are too many hidden sugars in processed foods, as well as that old enemy we now know to be salt.

22 Another Way We Can Be Influenced By Sugar

Mr. A., a triathlete, was a healthy looking man in his forties. He had his own business and could therefore devote a considerable time to his weekly training. With slight embarrassment he confided that he had a problem with sweating. In fact his wife had to change the bed every morning. He also admitted that he sweated greatly when he trained and that his sweat had a very strong pungent smell.

After listening to the details of his lifestyle I realised Mr. A. had an unusually good balanced diet. Generally he avoided sugar.

'What about fruit?' I asked.

'At least 6 pieces a day,' he said.

I suggested leaving out the fruit altogether for one week to which he agreed.

A week later he admitted in excitement, 'After three days my wife has only had to change the bed every second day!'

'You'll have to leave out fruit for quite a while. Eventually introduce just one piece at a time,' I suggested.

Fructose and other sugars, as mentioned before, can create too much acid in the body. In Mr. A.'s case, the acid was eliminated via the skin, particularly during the night and at training sessions. The strong smell occurs when there is dehydration in the body due to training hard and sweating, losing water out of the system, and then exacerbating the problem by not drinking enough water.

Mr. A. totally recovered. He had one other vice in his life: he consumed thirteen cups of sugarless tea a day. I suggested trying one week without the tea to see how it affected him. He complied.

The following week he confessed, 'I lasted three days and had a bad headache. After half a cup of tea my headache went.'

That is a classic case of addiction. Often a reduction in intake will solve the problem.

23 Sugar And Hot Flushes?

I was well beyond the change of life (menopause) but I had faced it without the use of HRT and with hardly any changes to my lifestyle. I remembered that my mother had suffered from hot flushes greatly but I seemed to have escaped them.

A few years into my change of life my husband and I went to our caravan in Cornwall. We enjoy surfing, weight training and walking across the landscape. We often find ourselves a little country restaurant and have a wholesome meal.

The guesthouse we found on this day made homemade apple pie, custard and ice cream - my favourite pudding! As I was looking at it longingly my husband suggested, 'one won't hurt', so I gave in to my desire.

The following day we ended up in the same restaurant again, eating the same dessert. Needless to say, we repeated it five days running, until we returned to London.

I had not consumed sugar in any way or form for a very long time. The sudden intake of the sugar rich dessert fostered my craving anew. As soon as we arrived home I introduced one honey sandwich a day into my diet, for a whole week. It happened almost automatically.

As soon as I started work again, one day after arriving back, I suffered a major hot flush. Shortly afterwards the same thing started to happen repeatedly. It lasted throughout the first week back, and then the following one.

I ate the honey sandwiches for just one week.

Immediately my hot flushes stopped. I was thrilled.

One month later we went to Cornwall again. Every day I had my favourite pudding as before. As soon as we arrived back the hot flushes began again. This time I did not have any honey sandwiches. At the end of the week my hot flushes subsided.

The following month we found ourselves in Cornwall again. This time I had the same dessert for five days, this time deliberately. I realised that the sugar intake led directly to hot flushes. The theory was now proved.

As soon as we arrived home I had the expected result, a week of hot flushes.

Many women suffer from hot flushes and take HRT for it. Maybe they should look to their sugar intake instead. I would. It may well be worth it!

24 Back Pain And Allergies

Mr. C. suffered from chronic back pain. He had osteopathic treatments, deep tissue massage. He changed his diet and moved to no sugar and no alcohol, instead introducing slow burning carbohydrates and salads as well as protein. It did not improve his back problem in the slightest.

Mr. C. changed his chair and his working habits, again without any positive results. After months of treatment he was finally admitted to hospital and put on traction for three weeks. Again no improvement followed.

Mr. C. was desperate. Nobody seemed to be able to help him. Another two months went by. On one particular day he telephoned and begged me to help him with massage. He could not get out of bed as his whole back had seized up.

When I applied a deep massage to his very tight muscles I had the impression that his whole system was poisoned. As this happened a long while ago I had only just passed my massage course and I could not understand why I felt he was totally polluted. Every muscle in his body seemed over-trained yet he did not exercise. I also knew as I was treating him that all I was doing would not make the slightest difference to his condition.

At the end of the massage he still felt the same as I knew he would. Unfortunately I had to leave him like that and went home.

A few months later he suffered greatly with terrific migraines in addition to the bad back. We did not work on Saturdays but he rang and begged my husband to do something. My husband worked on his upper back and neck for a length of time but still to no effect.

As Mr. C. was sitting on a chair resting, I offered him a cup of tea and asked if he took milk. On an impulse I went on to question him about how much. 'A pint and a half daily' he admitted. I thought it to be excessive and recommended that he cut it out for a week. This is known as an exclusion diet. 'It is important to know whether you'll feel worse or better without drinking milk. If there is no change in your condition, milk is not affecting you and you can continue drinking it.'

After only three days of abstinence Mr. C. rang me very excitedly, 'I feel so much better. I'll never drink milk, or anything to do with milk, again. My whole family is off milk now!' He just could not get over his improvement.

I never realised before how much a food item we love, and eat a lot of, can influence us in body or mind.

It takes me on to another story in which a girl suffered whenever she ate cheese.

25 Dairy Products Versus Body/Mind

Miss Y., a 19 year old lady, suffered from hallucinations and nightmares. I went through the routine questions with her, concerning body and mind. When I asked her about milk, she said she couldn't stand it as it made her feel sick. However, she loved cheese. I sensed my analytical warning light illuminate.

I suggested she try one week without any dairy products at all. Her face dropped. It really seemed like it would prove a major problem for her. 'I eat cheese every day. How can I replace it for a whole week?'

When someone protects a food item by making excuses in its favour, it usually signals an addiction. Nevertheless Miss Y. was cooperative and agreed to eliminate cheese from her diet for a week.

At the next appointment she exclaimed excitedly that after only three days her hallucinations had subsided and after the week without dairy products her nightmares discontinued. She could not believe it!

Thinking about my own diet, I realised how much cheese I had been eating recently. A few months previously I had started eating vegetarian cheese which had seemed to agree with me, as normal processed cheese gave me unpleasant after effects. Gradually I introduced vegetarian cheese every day into my diet although in small amounts.

Shortly after I started eating the cheese my breasts became very sore. If somebody brushed past me I automatically protected my upper body with my arms, hoping nobody would notice. I thought it to be a late part of the menopause which I had been through some five years previously without any disturbing effects.

The soreness in my chest prevented me from being able to lie on my stomach on a hard floor, which I often need to do when exercising. I now had to support my chest with a soft pillow underneath. However, once I had eliminated the cheese from my diet, my bust was less painful after just three days. Within a week I was able to lie on my stomach without discomfort.

There is a simple rule: if you think a food item is affecting you in an unpleasant way, then take it out of your diet for a week. If there is a noticeable difference, for better or worse, leave it out for good. Otherwise you can continue with it; this is a procedure known as elimination diet.

Generally speaking milk, as with any dairy product, contains lactose plus the enzyme 'lactase' which helps with digesting the lactose. Milk is pasteurised by law to kill off the bacteria that cause tuberculosis. 'Pasteurised' means it has been heated to 80 degrees centigrade, which unfortunately destroys the lactase enzyme in the milk leaving the lactose behind. Some people, often babies, are sensitive to pasteurised milk, and it causes them stomach problems.

26 Quantity Is Irrelevant

Miss P., a 23 year old student, suffered from an allergy to alcohol. During her time at university, and possibly even before, she consumed large quantities when socialising, especially at parties. The symptoms of the allergy had manifested themselves as an extreme cold, which she found difficult to shake off.

Miss P. had now not touched alcohol for the past two years. On one particular Sunday she went to a church service with friends. When they all decided to take communion, she wanted to take part as well. As soon as she had the smallest sips of the wine the vicar offered to the congregation, she started having a sneezing fit.

On return to her seat she suffered from a runny nose and streaming eyes. Her sinus system flared up instantly as it had not done for years. She jokingly suggested, 'I might as well have had the whole bottle of wine; it couldn't have affected me any worse!'

Once allergies have established themselves in people, a tiny amount can trigger off large scale symptoms. If a reformed alcoholic drinks even the slightest amount of alcohol it can lead to them starting the habit and therefore the addiction all over again.

Just to remind the reader: Alcohol is made from sugar and the addiction is related to the blood sugar level in the body. When the level goes up one feels good; when it drops one feels exhausted. If it rises too quickly in the blood stream, the pancreas will overcompensate and make too much insulin, just in case there is another high intake of sugar to follow. This leaves the sugar level low, which in turn can lead to mood swings.

27 How Does Sugar Affect Children?

James was an intelligent five year old. His parents were very proud of him. He was their only son, and consequently a little spoiled, but he enjoyed going to school.

Recently he had been behaving rather strangely and out of character. Everyday after his school lunch, he had started picking fights with one of the children there. The headmaster telephoned the parents who were completely bewildered by his behaviour. They questioned James but the child did not have an answer for what he'd done.

After seeking help from various places, the parents eventually found a nutritionist who assessed James's diet. It was found that he was addicted and allergic to all kinds of sugar: sucrose, glucose and fructose, as well as foods which contained hidden sugars, such as tomato ketchup and baked beans. He could not tolerate additives, colouring or stabilizers either.

James's parents knew this would ultimately mean no school dinners, no fruit, sweets, chocolates, sweet soft drinks or dried fruit. They explained to James carefully and in detail how these foods affected him. They made a deal with him, that if he took a packed lunch to school every day and ate what they told him to eat, there would be a present for him at the end of each week. He also had the choice of saving the money in order to buy something at a later date instead.

Thankfully he agreed. He took sandwiches to school which contained protein and salad. The lunch was varied to make it more interesting. All meals were tailored to his diet: For breakfast, porridge and some herbal tea. Fruit juices and Ribena were discouraged. They introduced some nuts in the afternoon and dinner without dessert was on the menu in the evening. Just before bedtime he could have some more porridge if he wanted it or maybe a sandwich if he was hungry. James improved greatly. His attention span was very good. He was quiet and polite while at the same time he had fun with his friends.

Then a few months later, out of the blue, the headmaster telephoned James's parents to report he had beaten up a pupil again.

His parents were devastated. 'Why?' they asked him, when he arrived home. He confessed that one of his friends, who also took a packed lunch to school, had asked him to exchange one of James's sandwiches for the other boy's grapes. They had provoked an immediate reaction from James, who became so agitated that he had to hit somebody.

28 Sugar And Animals

Our lop ear rabbit Sandy was a few months old when we began to allow her to stay in our conservatory overnight. Her bed was a little shoebox filled with straw, which she seemed contented to sleep in. On the coffee table I had arranged a large bowl with fruit.

The following morning I noticed that our rabbit had eaten her way through a banana, starting with the peel. She had consumed quite a large section of it. However, there did not seem to be any harm done, apart from a little diarrhoea. From thereon Sandy developed a liking for anything sweet. She would sometimes have a piece of my daughter's jam sandwich. She also liked honey and other sweet fruit. Our tortoise, our rabbit and the birds in the garden all liked the breakfast cereal Alpen. In those days I did not know how badly sugar could affect living creatures.

Sandy became a very large rabbit and quite fat, as you can imagine. She suffered from constant diarrhoea and was always hungry. By now her diet was varied and she loved dandelion leaves.

As Sandy grew older, not only did she suffer from irritable bowel syndrome but also her hip became arthritic due to the extra weight. It just shows how even animals can be affected by too much sugar and a 'fast food' diet.

29 Triggerpoints

What are they?
When do they occur?

Any substance which initiates a function is known as a 'trigger'. In physical therapy, especially in deep tissue massage, the points which trigger a feeling of burning, the sensation of a needle prick or that of being knifed, are called 'Trigger points'. These unpleasant feelings often radiate deeply into the body, especially when it's disturbed by external pressure. They can also spread upwards, sideways and diagonally. In severe cases they even appear in another part of the body. These trigger points are mainly found on the back, in between the shoulder blades, in the back of the neck and occasionally on a nerve root. They are usually found amongst chronically tight muscles and can appear anywhere in the body.

Within tight muscles blood circulation is restricted. Blood feeds and bathes muscle fibres. When a person's diet is rich in waste products, pollution is created in these tight areas. Small crystals can appear consisting of waste. When these trigger points are disturbed by pressure, during movement or a treatment, they radiate pain. Often these powerful trigger points contain strong emotions as well. Here are some evidential case histories:

Sandy, a forty year old divorcee, suffered from tension in her back. It was her first deep tissue massage. Sandy seemed a placid, happy go lucky lady. She had a new partner and everything in her life appeared in order.

During the massage we stumbled onto some nasty trigger points in the rhomboids (shoulder area). When being worked on, they beamed out pain into different directions. I pressed my finger deeply into the most painful point and stayed on it, until I felt it slowly releasing. During the session I explained that sometimes old emotions can be trapped inside these points. They need releasing because they can leave remnants behind. The person could suddenly suffer from anger or guilt or other emotions, whatever they had experienced sometime in their life before.

After the treatment, Sandra took the bus home. At the following session she could not wait to tell me what had happened to her.

'After I left you I got onto the bus and sat in the back. The bus was about to pull away, when a man just about managed to get on. The bus driver pulled away and almost made the passenger fall over. The passenger got very cross and shouted at the bus driver, who had to stop the bus. The passenger carried on telling him off.

'At that moment, I got up and went towards the man. An overwhelming feeling of anger went through me. The passenger was double my size. It did not make the slightest difference. I was ready to lay into him in no uncertain terms. From the bottom of my heart I screamed at him and ordered him not to talk to the bus driver like that. I then commanded him in terms I'm not going to repeat to leave the bus at once.

'The passenger faltered, complaining to me that the driver should not have pulled off so jerkily.

'Off the bus!' I shouted. The passenger got off the bus.

Everybody clapped. As I sat down I suddenly realised what I had done. I felt embarrassed. It all seemed to happen in a kind of a daze.

'Did your ex-husband bully you?' I asked.

'Yes, he always shouted at me. I used to be scared of him,' she said.

'Did you not speak up for yourself when he shouted at you?'

'No, I did not have the courage.'

'You must have been very angry with him at times.'

'I was, for years.'

'Well,' I said laughing, 'You told him off 'good and proper' this time; and the passenger will never behave like that again!'

The whole episode had proved very cathartic. The release of trigger points prompted emotions such as anger forward from the long term memory into the short term memory, then to be released.

30 Granddad

another Trigger Point story

On our return from holiday my husband, the children and I heard about Granddad's heart attack. When we visited him in hospital, he looked sick and pale. After a week he recovered sufficiently to be allowed home.

A while later we started Granddad's weekly massages on my couch. As I approached the left upper part of his back I pressed on a massive trigger point in the left rhomboid in between the left shoulder blade.

'That's exactly the pain I suffered when I went into hospital with my heart attack!' he called out. I pointed out that I was pressing on a trigger point and asked him where the pain I was releasing travelled.

'Straight into my heart area.' Granddad was very excited.

'When I let go of the trigger point, do you still feel the pain anywhere?' I asked.

'No. Nowhere.'

Pressing on that same point again, I asked, 'Do you feel anything now?'

'Yes, the pain is going through my chest into the heart area.' I released the trigger point.

'How does it feel now?'

'No more pain!'

He then told me that, in the ambulance on the way to hospital, they had given him a tablet to put under his tongue for the heart attack. The tablet had made him very ill at the time. When he had recovered after about five days, he did not dare complain about pain in his heart area any more in case they gave him another pill.

After his release, he had still suffered the same pain as before he went into hospital, until the trigger point was released.

It just shows you can learn something new every day. I certainly did not connect pain in the chest or even symptoms of a heart attack with trigger points.

31 Triggerpoints And Sciatica

Pain down the sciatic nerve is usually due to a space occupying lesion in the neural foramen, which is where the nerve exits the spinal column and travels down the leg. On some occasions it can be because of tightness in one of the deep muscles of the pelvis, the piriformis. Occasionally the nerve itself is swollen. Sometimes, hard though it might be to believe it, emotions can contribute to this pain.

After some heavy lifting, my husband developed severe sciatic pain. I treated his back, family members who were chiropractors treated him, but none of us made any progress on the problem. Doubled over, taking painkillers, my husband carried on working in our busy clinic. He was far worse than any of his patients. Especially during the night he would disturb me, calling out in pain. He asked me again to treat him. He could not stand the pain any more.

My final examinations in psychology at London University were due in a matter of days. I was about as stressed as I'd ever been. With a quiet internal prayer, asking for help, I wondered where to start. Nothing seemed to help. We had tried everything we could think of.

I asked my husband to lie face down on my couch. The pain was in his left lower part of his back in the gluteals and down the whole of his leg. I put my hand, at random, half way up the calf muscle, and my husband screamed in pain.

'Stay on that spot, that's going all the way up to my back,' he said.

I kept the pressure on and released the trigger point which had formed on the pathway of the sciatic nerve at that level. The sciatica went away as fast as it had arrived.

A strange thing about our bodies is the area where the symptom is felt is not necessarily where the injury originates from, so it is important to determine the cause if at all possible.

32 True Sciatica

One Christmas morning early, the doorbell rang. A man stood there on the doorstep, doubled over in pain. He had sciatica all along the nerve from the lower back to the lower part of his leg. My husband examined him and it turned out to be true sciatica, neuralgia of the nerve itself, due to severe mental stress.

At the end of the treatment the patient received gentle electro-magnetic treatment. As he lay there I had time to talk to him asking when the pain had started. It had hit him that very morning, his first Christmas on his own without his wife and children who had moved away pending their divorce.

Unfortunately anything related to emotional stress suddenly manifesting itself into physical pain is usually very slow to heal. The patient needs to change his attitude towards the stressful situation, looking at a more positive outcome.

33 Back Pain Due To What?

A middle-aged lady suffered from general back pain. It was hard to locate, as it travelled continuously to different areas of her back. She only responded on a short-term basis to all physical treatment given; deep tissue massage had the same limited effect. Even hypnosis only helped up to a point.

Each time the lady arrived for her next appointment, she told us the same story. In the meantime two and a half months went by and we had still not made any further progress.

'When exactly did it start?' I said, wondering whether to go through the consultation again with a fine toothcomb in case we had missed something.

'I can tell you exactly when the pain started, three days after I started with my HRT.'

'I guess these are not the right tablets for you,' I said. 'Can you consult your GP and maybe change tablets or the dosage?' She agreed.

The following week she smiled, 'I am so much better.'

'What is the reason?'

'I've only been taking my HRT tablets every other day.'

I urged her again to consult her medical doctor about it. The following week she telephoned, 'I have no pain at all anymore. I've now stopped my tablets completely and will never take any of those ever again.'

What had I suggested? That she should consult her GP. But the decision was entirely hers and I think she made the right one for herself.

I need to point out that back pain is obviously not always related to what you eat, drink or ingest; it can have many different causes. What I have noticed over the past twenty-five years of practice is that when the pain does not stay on the same side of the body but travels from left to right, or when it is felt on both sides of the body equally, mental stress and the wrong diet are often more likely to be the cause.

When the pain stays on one side only, particularly on the dominant side, it is generally more wear and tear related. The treatment differs accordingly.

Generally treatment will not last, only effecting improvement up to a point and relapsing quickly when the cause is not understood and therefore eliminated. We need to focus on what a person eats, drinks, breathes in, and whether they are continuing with the same work or hobbies that perhaps started it in the first place. Stress will always put the lid on the whole situation and make it deteriorate further.

34 Chronic Sciatica Or Anger?

Mr. Z., about 60 years old, had suffered from severe sciatic pain for quite some time. It had slowly worsened until he felt unable to stand it any longer. Osteopathic treatment and deep tissue massage did not bring the desired results.

I have often found that when physical treatment does not work it is time to look at the why, when, what, where and how of the condition. After listening to this case history I opted for a hypnotherapy session. Mr. Z. complained about how his family had treated him over the years. He lived with them and his anger had grown day by day. He defended his corner and there were many shouting matches.

As he gave me more details and mentally relived these, his back pain had increased considerably. I had to take special care to put him into a position where he was out of pain during the hypnosis. That meant he had to lie on my couch, facing the wall. The way the couch was positioned meant I was now sitting behind him, which could not have been any more awkward.

As usual I sent my thoughts out asking for extra help from the universe. I believe in what I work with and tell people so since there is no point lying to myself or anyone else.

Mr. Z. was soon in a deep trance. As he liked gardening, I described a beautiful place with many flowers, trees, birds and butterflies. The sky was blue and the sun was shining brightly. I asked him to lie on the grass and to feel the energy of the grass penetrating his body. I highlighted sensations of happiness surging through his body and mind, making him feel high-spirited. The sunshine in the sky became the golden white light in the universe. This light then represented unconditional love. It incorporates forgiveness, self-forgiveness and protection. All the wisdom of the universe is part of the light and it also stands for the ultimate truth, which can be totally trusted.

I continued assuring him that feeling saturated with love, understanding and gaining a deeper awareness and that he was now ready to forgive himself for what he had done and should not have done, or what he should have done and did not do. It was all in the past now and therefore outdated and unimportant.

He was also ready to forgive others for what they had done to him, or what they hadn't done and should have.

I urged him to keep breathing in the light with its unconditional love, at the same time letting go of all negative feelings such as anger, guilt or anything that he wanted to add himself. He was now putting himself in a bubble of light and love. It stood for safety and security and was his ultimate protection. Anything that came with love from the outside could penetrate the wall of the bubble and connect with him. He could send love from the inside to the outside. He could fight his battles with love. Nobody can beat Love!

It meant that all the home-made shields, walls, fences and defences he had created for his protection in the past were outdated and could now be taken down. They isolated him from others. If he sent love and forgiveness to his family, they would change.

When I woke Mr. Z. up, I asked him how his sciatic pain was and he pronounced it as having improved. However he could not wait to tell me that there was no way he could forgive his family for all of what they had said and done, though perhaps he could forgive them a little of it. Letting go of all his anger would leave him defenceless. He estimated he could drop sixty percent of it, which I pointed out would still leave him with forty percent of back pain!

35 Reflexology

When I qualified in basic massage, one of the first things I bought to hang on the wall in my surgery was a reflexology foot chart. It was colourful and jolly and had caught my eye. It wasn't that I wished to qualify in reflexology, as frankly I did not believe in it.

During a foot massage, one of my patients complained about an uncomfortable sore area under the sole of his foot. Eager to use my new chart to locate what the area stood for, I told him that according to the reflexology chart, it corresponded to his lung and bronchial area. He then told me that he suffered from asthma, which I found curious.

Another patient had received a physical treatment for cerebral palsy. With each treatment his walking had progressed, so much so that he became worried about losing his disability pension as he was only allowed to walk so many steps from his car unaided, and he had now advanced well beyond that limit.

During a foot massage I had noticed a tiny pimple as small as a pinhead underneath his foot, in the centre of his big toe. I pressed onto this point as hard as I could until he began to yell. Without looking up I asked him if the pain was in his foot.

'No, in my head!' he shouted.

I noticed that he was holding his head in both hands.

'Amazing,' I thought.

I have still never studied reflexology myself, but I certainly now have a much greater respect for it.

36 Abuse and Reflexology

An attractive forty-year old lady received deep tissue manipulation for her painful back. During the consultation she confided in me that her entire family had been abused by their father. It was from the age of five that she had personally been sexually abused. She loathed her father. Yet when he died she was compelled to go to his graveside, and actually mourned him.

She continued, saying she did not know what love was. Her father was only ever loving towards her when he abused her. She had no idea how to behave when she had her first boyfriend. When anybody hugged her she identified the experience with the same situation she had suffered with her father.

Each session she repeated the same story. The tone of her voice and her behaviour were very much that of a victim. She tended to blame others for the plight in her life now. With compassion I acknowledged her suffering, suggesting that as it couldn't be changed it would be best to move on and not run the risk of trying the patience of her partner with the story.

I encouraged her to imagine an almost new car that belonged to her. Suddenly somebody comes along and scratches it. She as the owner, would be understandably upset at the time, but would be relieved to realise later that she herself was actually unhurt.

'That is how I want you to look at your life now. You are a spirit with a body. Your body was abused but your soul, the real you, is fine.'

'Funny, you should say that,' she said. 'When I was abused I seemed to detach myself from my body. It would always seem like I was in the corner of my room watching what was happening. I have always wondered about that.'

When I was massaging her foot, and touching her big toe, she suddenly informed me she had forgotten to mention that there was no feeling in either of her big toes. In reflexology the big toe represents the head. I began squeezing the worst toe of the two as hard as I could; after a short time she felt something. The sensation increased. The other big toe received the same treatment with the same response: she actually now felt pain where it had been previously numb.

From that time onwards she felt much clearer in her head, she confessed. Most importantly, she never repeated the same story anymore. She was ready to move on.

37 Charlie's Vision

At the beginning, Charlie worked for us as a gardener. He used to come once a week to tidy up our premises. I did not know him very well, although later he became a very good friend to us.

I was busy as a physical therapist and badly needed some help in the house, particularly with the vacuuming. One November day I plucked up the courage to ask Charlie whether he would be interested. I was concerned that it might have been too much for him as he was in his late sixties. He also worked as a gardener for other people.

Charlie was only too pleased to help. I slowly went up the stairs to show him around the house. He followed behind. Halfway up I suddenly stopped. A thought came to my mind and I had to tell him. I knew that his wife had passed away ten years before. He still talked about her and looked after her grave meticulously. He missed her very much.

I told him not to go to the cemetery and put flowers on his wife's grave as she wasn't there. She had to make the same effort to get there as he did. I urged him to pick flowers from his garden and place them next to his wife's picture, to talk to her and send his love, which she would certainly get.

Charlie had listened carefully. Then he assured me he would do that in future but he had been to the cemetery only the day before and had planted flowers on her grave as that day was their wedding anniversary: The 11th day of the 11th month at 11 o'clock had been their day, many years ago. I wondered why I had picked that day 'accidentally' to tell him about his wife's grave.

During the week I did not see Charlie. One of my husband's patients whom I had never met before gave me a primrose in a tiny pot. I admired it and asked why she had given it to me.

'I don't know,' she answered, 'I went to the green grocer and felt that I had to get it for you.'

Wonderful, but how strange, I thought.

A week later Charlie returned. He was excited, and keen to talk.

'Have you been working with me, Mrs. Pearce?'

'How do you mean?' I said.

'When I went home that last day I saw you, I saw a flower in my garden which I picked and put it in a small glass of water and placed next to my wife's photograph, like you said. I talked to her and kissed the picture good night as usual. Then I went upstairs and opened my bedroom door.

'Immediately I saw a half circle of golden stars in the middle of the room. I started wiping my glasses but nothing changed. I switched off the light but the stars were even brighter in the dark for about ten minutes. I was in shock.'

He had concluded that I had asked him to put the flowers next to his wife's picture and so I must have made that happen. He also explained to me again, that the day I told him about not putting flowers on his wife's grave he had indeed put primroses on her grave, because her name was Rose, shortened from Primrose.

I showed him the pretty primrose I had been given. We looked at each other silently and I said, 'Thank you, Rose!'

38 My Vision

At 'Burrows Lea'

About 20 years ago my friend and I went to Burrows Lea, a former stately home, belonging to the healer, Harry Edwards. Earlier I had read a book about healing written by the same author, who had passed away about twenty years before. He so beautifully described his healing sanctuary and grounds that I had always promised myself to visit it when I had the chance.

My friend and I arrived one Thursday, half an hour before opening time. It was February and a particularly cold day. To pass the time in the car park on the premises, I suggested we do a meditation. It was our very first attempt and I instructed her using the method I had read about in a magazine.

'You close your eyes. Then visualise a white screen. From memory you then transfer your house onto the screen and see what happens from there.'

My friend listened carefully and closed her eyes. Within thirty seconds she started snoring. All I will say in her defence is that she was a pensioner.

Closing my eyes did not enhance my relaxation. It seemed to magnify the cold, although I wore gloves and boots. My gloves seemed to disturb my concentration somehow, so I took them off. I rested my bare hands in my lap, opened my eyes again and stared into the evergreen hedge.

Concentrating on one leaf only, my eyes began to water. I had to close them. I instructed myself to put a white sheet in front of me. And to my amazement, there it was! A bust of Harry Edwards appeared on the sheet from the right side. He looked much younger than I had seen him in my book; he appeared about thirty years old.

At the same time as the apparition, my hands heated up rapidly although I had shed my gloves; so did my feet and the tip of my nose.

I had no idea why the healer had planted himself on my white screen. I wanted my house to be cast on it. That is how the meditation had been described in the magazine. It also struck me as strange that I saw Harry Edwards at such a young age, when in the book I had read, he was in his sixties. How was it possible?

The vision must have lasted about two minutes. The picture of the healer faded away to the right, where it had come from. As soon as it vanished my friend snored particularly loudly and woke herself up. I told her about my vision. She was not very impressed. I think she thought that I had been dreaming. It was time to enter the healing sanctuary. We found ourselves in a grand library where I picked up a book, opening it at random. I could not believe my eyes when there was that self same picture of a young Harry Edwards that I had seen in my vision. I was so excited by now and talked about it loudly to my friend.

There was a man's voice next to me. He must have walked in without me noticing, and explained that on a given page there was a photo of Harry and him. 'We used to take the healers from the Philippines to the Continent together in the 1960s.'

'Who are you?' I wanted to know.

'I am Arthur Findley,' he said before giving me his card.

Later I went to one of his services in which he gave a speech about his past life. I wanted to know who he had received his information from. I later visited that lady myself.

39 Is Telepathy Possible?

Telepathy, mind to mind understanding… How can we know whether or not it really works?

About fifteen years ago I took part in a weekend lecture entitled Mind Control. It was introduced by a then well known (and expensive) American company. Two long weekends had been reserved for the comprehensive sessions. We learned the basic way of hypnotising each other in order to take part in the last, most difficult lesson, to prove telepathy existed. By this time I was already very doubtful about its credibility.

We had to find a partner, somebody we did not know, from all the participants. I ended up with an Indian girl who seemed very genuine and compassionate. It was explained to us that we needed to hit three different people's illnesses.

In my case, the Indian girl had to hypnotise me lightly. Then when she was satisfied I was sufficiently under, she had to concentrate on the first person on her list. Under no circumstances was she allowed to mention that person's illness. It was my job to 'guess' what illness the person suffered from. It went as follows:

The Indian girl described the first person on her list, a fifty year old lady. As she visualised the lady, she described her likes and dislikes and told me where she lived and some other details.

At the time I did not think that I was being hypnotised at all. I certainly did not feel very relaxed. The day had been hectic and too much material had been crammed into the lectures. Not to be a cynic, I made an effort to participate and rationalised in my mind and figured out that a 50 year old lady might be suffering from a bad back. I then described it to the Indian girl. She seemed satisfied and carried on with the next person on her list, an 81 year old lady whom I assumed from experience might suffer from swollen legs. Again the Indian girl seemed contented.

Her third person was a twenty-one year old man so I knew at once that I could not cheat. This man could be suffering from anything from a broken leg to mumps. I was wondering whether to guess my way through the procedure or own up to her. Before I could decide I started feeling very ill.

It seemed to me like the severest form of hypoglycemia, a classic case of low blood sugar. I started feeling hot and cold, also very dizzy. Thank goodness

I had a sandwich in my bag. Eating it would probably make me feel better.

With my eyes still shut as I was meant to be in hypnosis, I explained to the Indian girl how rough I felt: It frightened me how I had deteriorated in such a short period of time. I confessed I was going to open my eyes and have that sandwich.

The Indian girl quickly summed up the result of her experiment: The first person did indeed suffer from a bad back. The second person definitely had swollen legs. 'The third person had Aids,' she exclaimed. Then she left me to find my sandwich.

Still searching, her voice echoed in my head: 'Aids!'

I felt as if I had the symptoms of aids myself. Could it be that I had picked that up from him?

Realising that it was not my illness, I commanded it to go away. To my amazement it disappeared. I sat there in disbelief. I did not need my sandwich anymore; I felt fine!

I was under the impression that I had to guess the illnesses of the different people, or better, that I had to pick up on them from the lady who hypnotised me at the same time as she visualised and thought of each person in turn. It had never entered my mind that one could feel what is wrong with a person, and that that in itself is also a form of telepathy.

40 Telepathy And Sacral Cranial Therapy?

It was about 10.30 at night when I arrived home one particular evening. Suddenly I had a strong urge to ring my daughter in Bristol.

Kina was studying Ceramics at the University. She was very protective of her work. Particularly beautiful pieces were securely positioned on the top shelf in her room. She was quite reluctant to leave the house in case something might happen to the ceramics in her absence.

As I got through to her I immediately heard her scream, 'It's all gone, it's all gone!'

'What's all gone?' I asked frantically. She carried on screaming and did not seem to hear me. I repeated my question and begged her to talk to me.

Then she cried, 'The shelf collapsed and all my best work is smashed! It took me such a long time to make it.' By now she was hysterical. I asked whether she was alone in the house and insisted she called a friend over at once and ring me straight back as I was very worried about her condition. I had never known her behave like that before. I could not be with her for some time as I was in London, a two hour car ride away.

In the meantime my husband had arrived home. He had studied cranial sacral therapy. Beside myself with anxiety, I asked him if it was possible to do cranial work on a photograph and produced one of Kina, our daughter, for him. He had never done it on a picture before but now he held his hands over the picture with his eyes shut and concentrated on any energy coming from it. Suddenly very excited, he sensed a cranial rhythm and continued working on the photograph until he felt a much calmer sensation emanating from it. He concluded from it that she was now more in control of herself.

My husband had been inspired by this newly found technique and wanted to investigate further. He asked for more pictures. I picked up a magazine and he worked on photos of different people. He was quite uninterested in who he was concentrated on, only the results. The first picture was of Princess Diana. No energy at all! The next one was Frank Sinatra – negative again! Then a photo of a Pop Star made him exhilarated because he detected a rhythm. He carried on with other images of people. The results varied as before.

We were puzzled as to why he felt a cranial rhythm with some and not with others until the penny dropped. The people with negative results were actually deceased. The ones with a cranial rhythm were very much alive. My husband was elated and wondered whether this technique had ever been attempted before. It certainly merited further investigation.

There is a reason for everything: the fact that I had the sudden urge to telephone my daughter at exactly the moment the shelf had collapsed. Could that have been telepathy?

I also felt that after the ceramics had smashed, Kina was freed of her obsessive behaviour and of the unhealthy protection of her work.

If we had not sought desperately to help our daughter, we would never have had the experience of pictures of living people giving off energy.

41 Paralysis - Cranial Therapy – And Telepathy

Mrs. B. presented in our clinic with paralysis on her right side. She had suffered a stroke after she had had a brain tumour removed. Both tumours appeared at the same place, on the left side of her brain. She responded well to physical therapy and massage. She also responded the same way other paralysed people did: by falling asleep during my treatment.

This particular day, after the weekly session, I introduced a basic cranial technique. While the lady was in a deep sleep, I gently held the base of her skull (occiput) and concentrated on her cranial rhythm.

Being curious to know why she had suffered a tumour in exactly the same spot twice, mentally I asked her the reason – I repeated the thought and then left a gap in my mind clearing my brain and going blank for a moment. I decided that I would accept whatever entered my mind as I went blank as the lady's answer, and take it from there.

'It was empty and had to be filled,' was the only thought that involuntarily entered my head. I queried, 'What was empty and had to be filled?' as a throwaway answer. Slowly I woke the lady up.

As I was going to help her get up and get dressed, a nagging thought stopped me. My mind urged me to tell her what had come to me but I really did not want to.

Hesitantly I ventured to ask her what might be taken as a silly meaningless question, giving her the option to ignore it. She listened as I asked her if her life was empty and had to be filled.

She looked at me long and with pain. Then tears flowed down her cheeks. Her husband was always away on business around the world and her only son had left with his family to live in Hong Kong. Her first tumour was detected two years ago shortly after he moved.

Is it possible that our body acts like a child to our thoughts? If our life is empty and the emotion of emptiness is felt in the brain, does the body fill the gap with something, in this case a tumour?

42 Telepathy From Beyond The Grave?

My beloved mother passed away when I was 33 years old. My husband and I and our two children lived in a suburb of London, as we do now. As I was the only daughter of my parents and my father was not alive anymore, I had to fly to Germany to arrange the funeral. My youngest child was only two years old. For this reason I found myself with just four days to organise and dismantle my mother's household.

In Germany I took one of my mother's tranquilizers so I could sleep. At the funeral I made sure I did not cry by pressing my fingernails into the web of my hand. The physical pain counteracted my emotional pain. I feared that if I let myself shed any tears at all, I would never stop crying. I needed a clear head to make all necessary arrangements.

When I returned to England I experienced the same dream every night: I had to organise the entire funeral over and over again every night. At the same time I knew in my dream that I had already done it. This went on for about six weeks. Eventually I could not endure it any longer and opted for a little prayer: 'Please God, don't let me dream it again, I can't stand it anymore.'

To be honest I did not expect a great change. I just did not know who to turn to for help.

That night I had a very different, vivid dream. My friend, who is alive now, stood next to me. My mother, looking well and happy, stood opposite me. In excitement I pointed out my mother to my friend. I then noticed that my mother did not speak to me. As I tried to communicate with her I felt convinced she was asking me if I wanted to see where she was now. My Mum was talking to me telepathically and I understood! A strong feeling of total trust was released between us from me to her. I wanted to see her new home and was ready to accompany her wherever it would take me.

Within seconds I felt as if I was whizzing through space. Because it was so fast, you could also view it as being 'sucked' through a tunnel. Shortly afterwards we arrived at a huge wooden station, clean but bare. It struck me as strange that the walls were empty of advertisements. The large hall was filled with single people, seemingly in a hurry.

I looked around and immediately didn't like it there. There was no green, no water and no sunshine.

As soon as I had these private thoughts, the person next to me explained telepathically, 'You arrive here. Then you go to a different place, according to your spiritual development.'

Within seconds I found myself and my mother sitting on the grass in a place like Kew Gardens. The weather was beautiful. We were surrounded by wild flowers. In the distance was a river. One could see people happily communicating, telepathically. There was a feeling of total peace and relaxation, also total safety and contentment.

I must have spent hours there; it appeared timeless. Suddenly, deep inside I had an urge to return to my world. As soon as I felt this desire I found myself in that big station again. Many people were trying to find their way. They were all disconnected from each other.

I looked around and wondered how I could get back to my family. There was no train, boat or aeroplane. At that moment I noticed a man watching me. He was a long way away at the other end of the station. He seemed to be in charge. I understood was he was telling me telepathically that I was there now and could not go back.

An overwhelming feeling of responsibility towards the wellbeing of my children came over me. They were so young, they needed me. Panic-stricken I hung on to the person nearest to me and shouted, 'I must go back to my children!'

Instantly I had this experience of whizzing through a tunnel again and woke up in my bed.

The whole dream was so vivid. I will always remember it. I did not have that dream about my mother's funeral again. I also now knew that she was still around. One thing bothered me though, 'How did I manage to get back into my world?'

I told this story to quite a few people in the past and asked the same question over and over again. One day the answer came to me: 'One must ask for what one wants; wishing it is not enough.'

I also came to the conclusion that if you want to achieve anything you must first help yourself. Do as much as you can yourself, then ask for help with the last unachievable bit. It usually works. If you don't get it, there is always a reason for it. Either it interferes with your spiritual development here on earth or it is not the right time. Never turn bitter. It means you are on the wrong path for sure.

It does not matter how hard our lessons are in this life – how unfair they seem to be – how innocent the person may be, there is always a reason why it has to be experienced.

43 Luck, Hunches Or Guidance?

Shortly after my mother died I had to attend my son's Christmas Bazaar at his junior school. In a dazed state I passed various stalls. A little girl offered me some raffle tickets. Still in a sombre mood from the funeral in Germany, I was not interested and just declined, shaking my head.

I felt a little guilty and mean and bought one 10p ticket with the coin I found in my pocket. I could not be bothered to look for my purse in spite of the child being so polite.

Not long afterwards the raffle started. Needless to say, I won the first prize with my one ticket, a beautiful large china doll. The headmistress had personally dressed her up in a pink lacy outfit with matching hat.

'The doll has lovely large blue eyes just like my two year old daughter Kina,' I observed.

That was it. I knew at once that this doll was a present from my mother to my daughter for Christmas.

My mother had visited me during the last two years of her life and had looked after Kina for eighteen months when I was working. They became very close until my mother had to leave for Germany.

44 Luck, Judgement Or What?

I was driving my father-in-law's white Escort van one particular morning to collect a prescription from our local GP. It was nine o'clock and very sunny. Our doctor had his clinic near a large roundabout. Usually there was heavy traffic but by contrast that morning it was quiet on the road. In front of the doctor's was a small car park for about three cars. I was lucky there was a space and drove straight in.

My prescription was ready for collection and within minutes I returned to my car. Next to me was another parked car. The driver was at the wheel, waiting for his wife to return from the GPs.

I wondered if I should reverse into the main road. There was no traffic at all. It would be easy. I also realised that I had no windows in the back of my van to see if there was any traffic. I guessed it could be quite a while before the lady came out of the surgery.

Then a sudden decision came into my mind. I obeyed the silent command to wait. Soon the lady returned and climbed into her husband's car. I heard him start the engine and slowly drive into the road towards which he was facing.

At the same time I started turning my car slowly within the car park in order to face the main road as well. Then there was an enormous bang. I thought that I had hit something.

In horror I saw that a police car driving at about 70 mph had smashed into the man's emerging car. There had been no siren. A parked car had partially blocked the visibility of the main road. The man had had to drive halfway into the road to see what was coming. At that same moment the police car had arrived silently. It had been too late to stop. At full pelt they had smashed sideways into the man's car.

The police car had been going at such a speed that I witnessed the man's car, itself, jump across the road, through a fence and over five cars which were parked in the grounds of a factory. Starsky and Hutch would have been proud of such a stunt.

The policewoman who had driven the car was in tears. The three other policemen looked ghostly white but were unhurt. They blamed a car which was partly parked on the pavement for the accident. The man behind the wheel kept repeating, 'I'm dying.'

I could easily have had that same accident myself. What had told me to wait? Yet, it did not make me feel any better. I felt so sorry for that man.

45 Telepathy Or Astral Travelling?

One Thursday evening at eleven o'clock, I went to bed particularly tired. Soon I was drifting off.

Suddenly I heard a loud sobbing in front of me. I felt it externally, at about chest height. As it was dark around me I called out, 'Who is there?'

I waited anxiously. My heart was pumping fast. I was scared. Everything was still.

As soon as I opened my eyes in the dark the noise had disappeared. I staggered to the light switch and could not get downstairs quickly enough. Nervously I waited for my husband who was due to return at any moment. It definitely was not a dream. I had not experienced it in my head but outside of my body. I reassured myself as I waited in the dim light downstairs.

At this point I must introduce our gardener, Charlie. He was then about 80 years old. For years I had known that he was psychic. He often heard a female voice inside his head. He called her his 'guide' and she often told him something which at a later date, would come true.

Two days later I was still occupied with the crying incident that had interrupted my nodding off so profoundly. I confided in Charlie, trusting he would be able to contact his guide to find out more.

I instructed him to ask his guide whether what I had experienced on Thursday night was a dream or reality.

He assured me it was real. He told me it was a young lady, white, with no children. I replied, somewhat irritated, that the description didn't exactly narrow the field. 'She is your patient and will be with you in two days' time,' he said. I could not argue with that. It was a case of just wait and see. Needless to say, I could hardly wait.

The following day a childless white English girl turned up. She was quite tearful and I surmised it might be her but as she claimed she'd had a happy week I ruled her out.

The following day, the predicted day, a nineteen year old childless white girl appeared. I hesitated to ask her. By nature she was always happy and full of beans. Eventually I could no longer resist it.

'Have you been upset during the week by any chance?'

'Yes,' she said. 'Last Thursday night.'

'Have you been sobbing?'

'I was hysterical' she admitted.

'About 11 o'clock at night?'

'Yes, how do you know?'

I joked, 'Well, all I can say is if you wake me up at unsocial hours again I'll have to charge you double!'

Still puzzled, she laughed.

I wanted to know if she had thought of me when she was distressed.

She then told me the story behind it:

On that very Thursday she had lost her job. She had lived with three other friends in a big house in a good part of London, about one hour by car away from our clinic. As she had no savings she had no option other than to leave her house and relocate, but she had no idea where to.

With the prospect of no job and nowhere to live she had gone hysterical. At that point she thought of me as I had helped her before at a difficult time in her life with hypno- and psychotherapy.

She told one of her friends how she wished she could see me for an appointment, but how she had no spare money.' The friend reacted helpfully, offering her a voucher for one of my massages which had been her Christmas gift the year before.

Many thoughts went through my mind at once. I analysed them in turn.

How was the girl able to contact me telepathically?

Somehow we must have created an ideal interpersonal connection. I had emptied my brain slowly drifting into the alpha brain waves just before you enter deep sleep. She desperately wanted to contact me directing a strong charge of energy specifically towards me and the connection was established. Her thoughts reaching me I would consider as pure telepathy.

What explanation could one have for my feeling or sensing the girl sobbing hysterically in front of me, outside my body not inside my head, just before I fell asleep? Was it a case of 'astral travelling' or telepathy, or both?

46 Astral Travelling

Out of Body Experience

Mr. J. was one of my volunteers for past life regression. He was a middle-aged man who was curious about his past life. At the time I needed volunteers to judge for myself how credible or incredible it was.

I deeply relaxed Mr. J. using my usual induction: your body is feeling heavier and heavier… with every breath you take you'll go deeper and deeper into relaxation. Eventually I felt Mr. J. was deeply relaxed, enough to go backwards in time, going backwards in his life to infancy and, ultimately, the womb.

I suggested Mr. J. was entering an inviting tunnel, at the end of which was a light. Passing through that light would lead him into his past life. At this point I made Mr. J. aware of my voice and stressed that he would also speak.

Though deeply hypnotised, he still heard my voice. People usually talk very little in hypnosis: Often only 'yes' and 'no'. They are barely answering the question. Generally speaking, the more they talk in sentences, the less deeply hypnotised they are. One can also tell that way whether they are faking it or not.

'Mr. J., where are you?'

'I am tumbling.'

'What do you mean?'

'Tumbling.'

After a while I enquired, 'Is there any change?'

'I'm getting bigger and bigger.'

'How do you mean?'

'I am still getting bigger.'

Eventually he proclaimed, 'I am as big as the whole world!'

'What is happening now?'

'I am getting smaller.'

'Why are you getting smaller?'

'I am still getting smaller.'

'I am a nothing!'

At this point I asked myself what he was trying to tell me. Instantly the thought came to me: I my soul, my real me, am a light made of unconditional love. Everything that is to do with Love, I become connected to, I become part of. If I love people, animals, plants, I become huge!

When I don't like myself, see people as untrustworthy and take a dislike to them; if I judge animals as dirty and children as noisy, if plants are weeds and a nuisance, I become a nothing. I connect with nothing. I am not worth loving.

Mr. J. in the meantime progressed further in his hypnosis: 'What is happening now?'

'I am going up and up.'

'Where are you now?'

'I am in the universe. It is dark.'

'Are you floating?'

'No.'

Later he filled in the missing details. He remembered far more then he told me during the session. He explained that he stood on something firm but transparent. It felt similar to glass.

'You said that it is dark.'

'Yes.'

'Are there stars?'

'There are lights.'

'I want you to concentrate on your heart chakra in the centre of your chest where you feel Love.'

'Think of someone you love very much. Can you feel that love in the centre of your chest?'

'Yes.'

'I want you to magnify this love and send it to one of the lights.'

'...have you done that?'

'Yes.'

'Still sending the love to that particular light, tell it to come closer to you. Can you do that?'

'Yes.'

'Still sending the love, ask it to come as close to you as it can; then put your arms around it. Can you do that?'

'Yes.'

'Now ask it who it is you are tuning in with, and where you are.'

'Did you get an answer?'

'Yes.'

'What did you get?'

'I mustn't know and it is not my time yet!'

I felt then that we were trespassing. Slowly I got him out of hypnosis. He then told me that the light had a man's deep voice, polite but authoritarian.

As this was one of my very early past life regressions which turned out to be 'Astral Travelling'. I discussed it with my teacher who then explained various aspects of the subject to me.

47 Einstein's Universal Embrace

A human being is part of the whole, called by us universe, a part limited in time and space. He experiences himself, his thoughts and feelings as something separate from the rest – a kind of optical illusion of his consciousness.

This delusion is a kind of prison for us; restricting us to our personal decisions and to affection for a few persons nearest to us.

Our task must be to free ourselves from this prison by widening our circle of compassion to embrace all living creatures and the whole of nature in its beauty.

48 Telepathy Works With Healing

An elderly Asian lady had been coming to me for massage treatment for many years. Her husband had died and she had become very ill. At first I could barely touch her, she was so fragile. But session by session she became stronger, especially when I finished the treatment with a short healing session. She told me about her family and that one of her sons had died at the age of 17. She had been very close to him and missed him still very much after all those years.

One Sunday morning one of her sons phoned me frantically to tell me that his mother had been taken to hospital for open heart surgery. The operation was successful but her kidneys had stopped working. She was also very weak and it was touch and go. He said that she had asked for me. I was taken aback a bit. Thoughts were racing through my head about the logistics of getting to the hospital. I did not feel confident driving in London. All I could think of was playing for time to decide about what to do next. I suggested to the lady's anxious son that he ring me again in one hour. I also requested for his mother to 'tune in' with me in exactly half an hour's time for ten minutes. I told him exactly the time to do that, to which he agreed.

Still thinking, I must find a way to visit her, I also realised that I had to stick to my suggestion of the absent healing appointment, though I did not think that it could do much.

I sat down in my treatment room to say a short prayer asking for help for the lady. Then I closed my eyes, visualised the lady as I remembered her and started putting my hands around her head. Instantly I had an overwhelming feeling of static energy, a buzzing in my hands, coming from her head. It was quite unpleasant. Then I put my hands to the area were I pictured her kidneys and felt ...nothing. The area was dead. I asked the kidneys why they weren't working.

'It's all too much!'

The answer came clearly into my mind.

I immediately went back to visualising her head. Again I sensed an aggravating buzzing of the wrong kind of energy. I had felt this before when people had headaches or migraines. I wanted to know what was 'all too much'. Then the thoughts poured through my mind, seemingly coming from her.

'My parents, my husband, my son, and other members of my family who are on the other side want me to join them. My sons in this life, the rest of my family and friends want me to stay here. I am in the middle. It's like being in a 'tug of war'. It is all too much, it is too much agony.'

I told the lady in my mind not to listen to any of them but to make up her own mind. The most important thing was where she wanted to be.

At that point I stopped my healing session, bewildered about what had happened.

Exactly one hour after his first phone call, the lady's son rang me again. I had barely answered the phone when he announced he knew I had talked to his mother despite my protestations to the contrary and my assurances that I had not telephoned her.

He then explained that his mother had told him about our conversation. He mentioned the tug of war feelings and how tired she was of being in the middle, pressurised by both sides. He agreed with my suggestion, that he would let his mother make up her own mind about living or passing on.

I was amazed and shocked. Never in my wildest dreams had I thought that healing worked in that way; that one could use telepathy successfully and that distance did not matter at all.

I visited the lady that Sunday in hospital; she was in a semi-coma.

The following Tuesday her son rang me again and told me that her kidneys were working again. At the same time he was very much on edge. His mother had just seen paradise and told him it was beautiful. Then she said, 'I know what to do now. I am not deciding whether I go or stay, I will let Him decide.'

After what had happened between his mother and me telepathically, the son thought I could do anything, including talking to God. I laughed and suggested that if I could, so could he.

The outcome was that the lady recovered and still comes, as usual, for her weekly massage, looking and feeling good most of the time.

49 About The Aura

Everything, all matter, has an energy field. Stones, plants, flowers, trees, animals and especially people have an aura. Kirlian, a Russian scientist, was one of the first people to photograph this energy field and give it its name, 'Kirlian photography'.

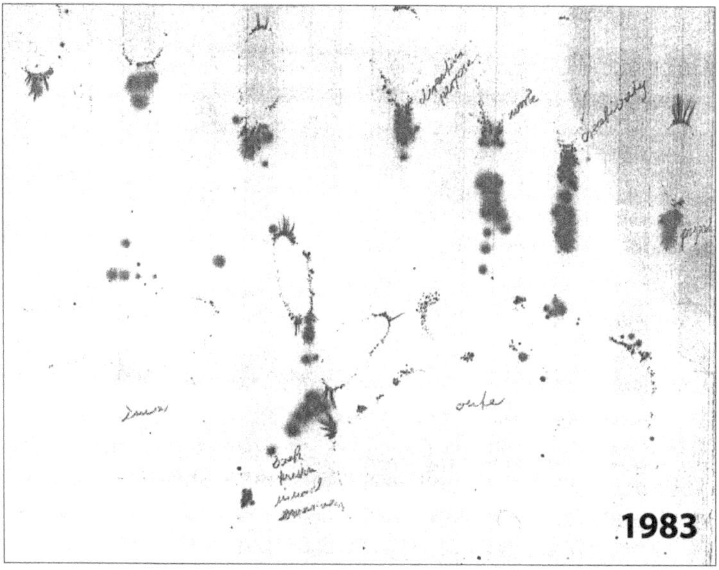

From the aura a healer can determine whether there is an imbalance, too much or too little energy, in certain areas of the body. A patient who suffered from a tumour on the brain was amazed when I could locate exactly the place where the tumour was situated. I could do that without touching just by feeling for the energy about two inches away from her head.

From these energy fields a trained person can determine whether a person is low on energy. See a Kirlian photograph of my hands in 1983 when my parents had just died and my life was chaotic. The blotches indicate blocked energy.

In 1988 the energy increased. It shows particularly as a corona around my fingertips. I actually made that happen by sending love, which I felt for my

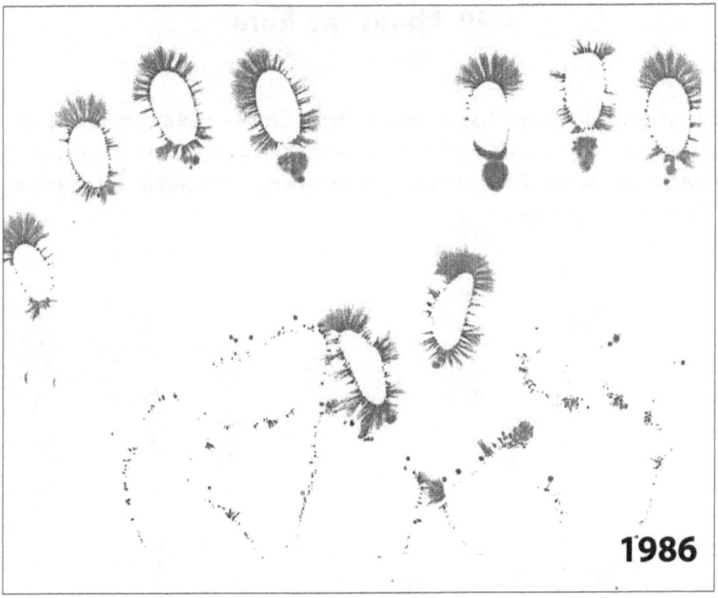

mother, from my heart centre, via my arms, into the palms of my hands. This made the energy of my hands increase considerably.

See the photograph of my aura in 1990. It is generally stronger but does not reach into my fingertips. Compare that with the photo of the hand of a healer during absent healing. Love is the highest spiritual energy or vibration. You can see that the healer used plenty of it. It also shows that I had only just started learning about healing.

Compassion, empathy, patience, tolerance and understanding are learnt usually through encountering hardship in life. It leads to self-awareness. Automatically our values will change as well: let us compare good times with bad times. What we call 'bad times' are actually the most valuable times for us. In those moments we learn the most. Often they lead to the most important spiritual examinations in life. Good times are enjoyable, but when they last too long one becomes bored, lazy and loses direction.

Most people marry partners who may seem totally unsuited. They seem to have nothing in common. External looks made them fall for each other. As stress and tension turn up in a marriage each partner wonders why they ever got married. They think that they have made a big mistake. At this point

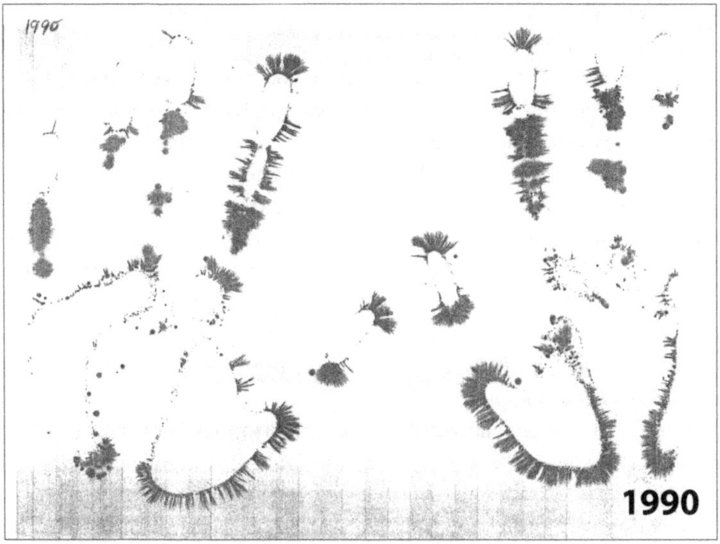

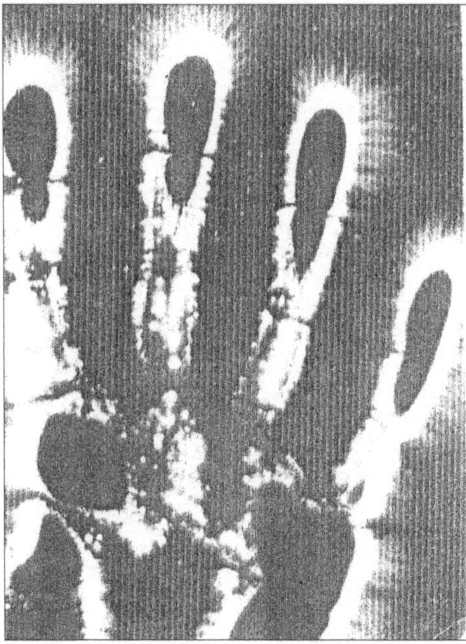

Hand of a Healer

During absent healing.
This specific blue appears particularly during healing processes

people often look at the option of separation, unfortunately.

Looking back on forty years of my marriage, I have experienced the difficulties one has to go through. Often the age between thirty-five to forty-five seems the worst. Judging by what we have in our marriage now: harmony, understanding, love, peace and fun, only because we stuck with it; we worked through it, we met half-way, eventually.

I advise strongly: Never think that you married the wrong person. There is a reason why a wife or husband might be a born victim or maybe a real dragon, a persecutor. There are reasons why we have certain hobbies, our phobias and fears or even continuous pain; nobody can explain. Even our traits and characteristics are often found in another, a former life or lives. I reached this conclusion after I performed many past life regressions. The outcome was sometimes mind-boggling.

When I learnt hypno- and psychotherapy and my teacher explained about past lives, I was not very happy. I used to feel relieved not to have lived in the Middle Ages, which I assumed must have been very cruel times.

Later I learned something completely different.

50 Healing And The Oak Tree

A famous healer taught me that love is the most important ingredient in healing. The idea is that the highest power, God, is pure Unconditional Love and Light. It stands for absolute Truth and can be completely trusted. This light also offers spiritual protection.

One cold winter's day I went on my own to Kew Gardens. The landscape was crisp; frost had painted a beautiful picture across the frozen lake and white lawn. It felt bitterly cold and the sunshine was missing. As I walked and watched hungry birds on the frozen branches of tall trees, I had a sudden thought.

When I learnt healing, I was taught that one could tune in with the energy of a tree. Since I seemed to be all on my own in the area of Kew Gardens, I chose a tall big oak tree. I lent my back against the freezing bark and put my bare hands, palms down against the trunk. All I could feel with my hands was the frosty bark of the tree. But this did not perturb me. I instructed myself to think of somebody I loved. Then, to feel that love in the centre of your chest (heart chakra). Now to imagine this energy of love advancing through your arms into the palms of your hands and then into the tree trunk.

I was still freezing cold. Yet with total discipline and determination, I continued directing myself to feel that love and to channel it through arms, palms and into the tree trunk. Then it struck me that as the tree was hibernating, its life force must be in the roots. So I soldiered on putting my love energy into the tree trunk and visualised it going into the centre of the trunk downwards into the roots.

I continued this for about two to three minutes. Then I felt that the tree owed me something. This was probably not the way to do it, but nevertheless, I asked the tree and I visualised its response to my request to channel its energy up its trunk into my hands.

Within about a minute I could feel my hands getting warmer and warmer and then really hot. I was stunned. This stuff works… Amazing! But nobody will believe me!

Then I got more brave and took off my shoes, putting one foot at a time against the tree trunk. They did not warm up, though I gave them the same determination and instruction I had used for my hands.

It confirmed that we can and are interconnected with all that is alive, on the love vibration. We hold the key to connect or not to connect. We have freedom of choice. For babies, small children in particular, as well as bigger ones, for animals and plants the currency is love.

That's how they value what they receive from us. Rational thinking seems to interfere or destroy that way of thinking, and values change.

51 Henry's Healing

A few years ago my grandson Henry, then 18 months old, went with the rest of the family to Germany. There was little time to see much and to meet a number of relatives. We also drove to my Mother's birthplace where we enjoyed a Christmas Market. We went shopping and finally ended up in a pleasant restaurant. We were looking forward to a substantial meal as we were all very hungry. As soon as we found a table, my grandson Henry started screaming. It had all been too much for him. I was given Henry to sit on my lap. Nothing could console him; that restaurant and all the people in it must have been the final straw for him; he could not take any more.

I thought to myself, everyone is tired from a long day of sightseeing and shopping. I'd better let my children, all grown-up, have a little peace and let them eat their dinner in comfort. I realised with a screaming child I would not be able to eat much of my meal.

I thought why not try my special way to sooth him. I had learnt how to do healing. It did not necessarily mean that I had to put my hands onto the baby but I could work on the aura, the energy field of the child. Maybe it would work.

My grandchild was lying on my right arm. I put my left hand about an inch away from Henry's head. Then I imagined Love flowing from my chest where the heart charka is, down my arm into the palm of my left hand and then connecting with Henry's energy field, one inch away from his head.

Within 30 seconds he went quiet. My daughter-in-law watched and must have wondered what was happening when Henry suddenly went fast asleep. I was speechless myself. I did not expect this response, certainly not going from a screaming child to one falling asleep within seconds. If I had expected this outcome, I would have asked my daughter-in-law for permission to do healing on her child. It was all so quick!

What it showed me was that babies and little children, also animals and plants, have a life force which is not 'blocked' by scientific thinking. I later realised that the older a child is, the more it thinks rationally and doubts things, the more the healing vibrations can be blocked.

52 Healing Works

My beloved lop ear rabbit, Sandy, developed an arthritic hip late in life, due to being overweight. She would sit quietly in the same spot, obviously in great discomfort. Over night I used to put her into a medium sized box with enough room for her to lie or sit in comfort, next to a dish of food and water. Every morning I saw to her food this way since she hadn't been well. She never lost her appetite, though.

After she had her food we used to have a short healing session, practising a skill I had just learned and was eager to use. I was never quite sure whether it worked at all and if it did, by how much.

During the healing session, both my hands were gently wrapped around Sandy's hips. I then focused on the area at the centre of my chest and imagined the love I had for my rabbit travelling from the centre, down my arms into my palms and then into her pelvis. Each time she totally surrendered into my hands. She certainly enjoyed the warmth and comfort it gave her.

One morning Sandy did not respond to my talking to her; also her favourite food had been ignored. She sat quietly in the far end corner of her box, looking very downtrodden. I knelt opposite her in front of the empty corner of her box, encouraging her to move. She made some high-pitched noises. Whilst talking to her I accidentally placed both my hands inside the box, palms towards her and found myself telling her I didn't know what she wanted or what she was trying to tell me.

With her back towards me, she suddenly wiggled her bottom backwards into my hands. I then realised that she was actually asking for healing. What more proof did I need that it works?

After our healing session which I gave with extra joy and compassion, she ate all her food and seemed much more contented. I could not believe how much she must have valued the healing each time, and how much comfort it must have given her. She just couldn't tell me in words.

53 Doing Things With Love

Through Matthew, a famous healer, I learned that if you could love enough unconditionally, you would be the most powerful person in the world. Try it. If someone is angry, retaliate with love!

It sounded really profound to me, a wonderful thought. But could it really work? Probably for others, but not for me, I concluded.

One evening I had to visit a friend. It was cold and dark. Snow covered most of the road I was travelling on. It was difficult for me to see the road markings. I believed that my road had the right of way and drove reasonably fast down the empty street.

Suddenly a car appeared out of nowhere from a side road, going at the same speed as me. The only difference was that car had right of way while I had not. We nearly crashed. I was lucky to be just in front of the car in time, so the collision was avoided.

Shortly afterwards I was at my destination and stopped outside my friend's house. The car I had avoided colliding with had followed me and stopped next to me in the middle of the road. I could feel the fury of the woman through the closed doors of her car. She had her mother and two children in the back.

Clearly seething, she got out of her car and charged towards me. She had left her car door wide open. I hesitantly wound my window down. I gathered that she wanted to talk to me. I didn't dare get out of my car.

Then she let rip, screaming that I should be locked up and not let out on the loose. I felt hurt as she also swore at me. I imagined her, from the way she dressed and her car, to be quite a refined lady normally. I searched for some suitably strong words to combat her verbal abuse. All I came up with in the event was, 'I'm sorry!'

They were like magic words. The woman looked at me, shocked. She then apologised profusely for her behaviour and asked me for forgiveness. I was speechless. What a change in a person!

Done with love, it really works. A triumph, indeed.

54 Do It With Love – This Time Telepathically

My husband and I had a heated discussion lying in bed after a long day's work. We disagreed and were quite angry with each other. My husband turned away from me and went to sleep.

I tried my hardest, but I could not sleep. It was most annoying. Then Matthew's advice, do it with love, entered my mind. I was lying on my back, visualising love. I could not get the feeling of love, as I was too angry. I imagined it like smoke coming from my heart chakra. Nevertheless, I put all the energy into the smoke standing for love. I visualised the smoke coming from the centre of my chest and travelling to my husband. After doing this for about ten minutes, I became tranquil and sleepy. I was just about drifting off, when my husband suddenly turned towards me and put his arm around me.

'It works!' I thought.

I was wide awake with excitement. My experiment proved positive. My husband would never have given in under normal circumstances.

55 Telepathy Or Intent? How Much Can We Influence Each Other?

Before I became a therapist, I attended a workshop run by a homeopath. My husband intended taking part but was unable to go, so I took his place. There were many different kinds of therapists present. I felt a little uncomfortable, as I knew none of these therapies at the time.

During a coffee break I found myself talking to a man who happened to be standing opposite me. I told him about something I thought might interest him. While concentrating on the details of my story I looked the man straight in the eyes, as I always do when I talk to people.

Within minutes I felt myself swaying, a motion that seemed to originate from deep inside my head. I unconsciously held on to the next chair not to let the man see me swaying. It became increasingly difficult to visualise details of my story, convey them to him and look him straight in the eye at the same time.

I told him I would have to look away while I talked, as looking at him confused me and made me forget the details of my story.

To my embarrassment he enquired whether I'd felt myself sway. Proudly he declared he was a hypnotherapist and he'd done it. Then he walked off leaving me with a hundred questions to ask him. How had he done that?

At the end of the workshop the homeopath, who was also a hypnotherapist, wanted to show his video about him hypnotising his daughter on TV. I was very interested and asked to see it too, though I wasn't a hypnotherapist. A voice behind me said I was but I don't know it yet. I turned around to find that man there again!

Years later, I worked as a hypnotherapist and specialised in Past Life Regressions.

I was explaining such a regression and how it worked to Charlie, our psychic gardener. He seemed fascinated by the subject. As he was listening intensely, his eyes connected with mine, in order not to lose me. Suddenly he could not look at me any longer and broke off. I asked if he was finding it difficult to follow me but he denied it. He later admitted that he couldn't look me in the eye for any length of time without going off to sleep.

I dismissed it as nonsense. To show him that he was wrong, I asked him to lie on my treatment couch and look me straight in the eye. Within seconds he was fast asleep. We tried this at various times and on different days. It sent him to sleep every time.

The following weekend we went to a family party. An eighteen year old relative stood next to me. We were chatting and laughing and I used the same technique on him with the proviso that I'd explain it all afterwards. All he had to do was look into my eyes. He did as he was told. Within thirty seconds he started swaying and his eyes were about to close. I insisted he opened his eyes there and then to which he complied, threatening never to look into my eyes again.

I tried it with more adult volunteers. The results varied.

With some people I could feel a built in resistance as I looked into their eyes. They were the mentally stronger kinds, these were more inclined to control others in real life situations, often without even realising it.

56 Purely Accidental?

One of my patients, Caren, asked me to accompany her to attend a group counselling session run by an elderly lady called Rosemary. It was a bright beautiful day and both of us had dressed up accordingly. By the time we arrived at the lady's house, they had already started. They were standing in a circle, meditating. Quietly I filled in the little gap between two people, finding myself standing next to the only man in the group.

Almost instantly he moved away from me in the opposite direction and carried on with his meditation leaving me to wonder whether there was something wrong with me, why he'd moved away and what everybody else might think about it.

Rosemary invited everyone to take their seats. She turned to the man and asked him to tell us his life story. He declined, despite his promise to do so and it being his turn to talk about the difficult times in his life.

'Not in front of her,' the man replied rudely, looking at me. I started feeling awful. Then a kind of an inner strength made me confront him.

'Why don't you want to talk in front of me?'

He protested that I had too much confidence.

'That's where you are wrong,' I argued.

Rosemary turned towards me, calmly.

'I know that you are new here,' she said. 'Why don't you tell us about yourself and the difficult times in your life?'

As a therapist I was reluctant to expose my downfalls in front of my own patient. My life seemed to rush backwards through my mind, stopping at the age of eight when my parents lost their business and we ended up virtually in the street. It was just after the war and there was not much accommodation available. They were such hard times, that my mother was contemplating suicide.

'That's not the answer!' the man shouted at me, so upset he started crying. 'My brother committed suicide.'

Then I realised why I had been picked on to talk. How amazing that I should unwittingly have mentioned the word suicide. It triggered the man's story, which he had not wanted to share with me.

The rest of the hour was filled with just his and my dialogue:

'Tell me more about your brother's suicide.'

'It's my fault. I might have prevented it somehow.'

'The last thing your brother wants, wherever he is now, is for you to blame yourself for the rest of your life. Your brother would like you to remember him in happier times. Things you used to do together matter. I believe that our spirit lives on. He would by now have learnt to view things differently. The advice from him to you would be: give your life a purpose again, be happy and do those things you used to enjoy. That would make him happy too.'

The man smiled faintly. It was a painful attempt.

'You have not laughed for a very long time, have you?'

'No,' the man agreed.

'I'll wager you read all the bad news in papers every day,' I said.

'I do,' he agreed.

'What did you used to like to occupy yourself with?'

'I loved music and played the piano. I also used to play cricket and was quite a sports person.'

'Would you be prepared to start that again?'

He nodded.

Rosemary reminded us that the time was up. We again formed a circle for our meditation. I looked at the man opposite me. He understood and moved himself next to me. His face had lit up. He was ready to step back into his life once again.

57 Telepathy And Faith

An Indian gentleman telephoned me to make an appointment for his wife who was in terrible pain with her back. As luck would have it I was able to give her an early appointment.

The day before I saw the lady I had been to my printer to fetch some professionally made leaflets. He would often have a little chat with me. He told me he had just printed a book about Sai Baba, an Indian Holy Man. He handed me a copy.

The lady I made the appointment for was indeed in great pain. She told me that she had undertaken treatment with many different practitioners. There had been little improvement and her husband was still very concerned about her.

During the hour long first session of treatment we formed a friendly relationship. She had found me in the Yellow Pages. She then told me about herself and her belief in Sai Baba. I showed her the book the printer had given me. She was pleased to see it and sensing that it meant more to her than it did to me I offered it to her. She accepted it with gratitude whilst at the same time confessing that she had not really found me in Yellow Pages. Rather her husband, desperately worried and determined to find the right therapist for her, had prayed to Sai Baba for help. He suggested in his prayer, that he would open the telephone book at random and stick a pin into the open page, with his eyes closed. He asked Sai Baba for guidance.

'You could have ended up with a plumber.' I could not resist joking.

To have such faith must be a wonderful thing.
I am still working on mine.

How often, when we are in trouble, do we send a thought out pleading with God to help us on the spot. When we look back at a later date, we find that we managed to scrape through.

If we feel we did not get any help at all, maybe we needed to suffer that lesson in order to learn from that experience. We usually end up a stronger person.

58 Ask The Universe!

A thirty year old, pretty lady had a problem. She was painfully shy. Her one male friend took advantage of the situation. He only invited her out when it suited him. The result was that the woman often ended up alone in her flat at weekends. Eventually she wrote him off as a waste of time. She confided in me, asking for advice on how she could meet a trustworthy boyfriend and if she did, how she would know whether he was the right one.

I explained that she'd know when she was in love. She wouldn't be able to leave him. He would always be on her mind. If the love was mutual, it would draw them together and they wouldn't be able to live without each other.

As the lady was a friend of mine, I suggested as an experiment we send a request into the universe. Nothing would be lost if it didn't work. She agreed.

Before I started the hypnosis I asked her for as many details as possible about what she was looking for in a future partner, looks, character and so on.

Soon she was in deep hypnosis. I realised that I first of all had to make her feel better about herself to boost her physical and mental energy.

'Imagine you are inhaling the healing colour blue with its balancing vibrations, along with a golden white light,' I suggested. I then asked her to welcome these colours into all parts of her body and mind. I emphasised that it stood for unconditional love, forgiveness, and anything she might want it to be, provided it enhanced her body, mind and spirit.

I continued urging her to see in her mind's eye the light penetrating through the pores of her skin, feeling it enter her blood supply, nerve supply and lymph supply; to sense it now advancing into her bones and bone marrow and into all the organs of her body.

I told her, 'You can feel the warmth, the glow, the energy and the compassion balancing and harmonising your entire body, including your conscious and unconscious mind.' I stressed that the conscious mind was becoming more constructive, especially the area where her thoughts were being formed. I stressed that she was in charge of these thoughts, that she could change or eliminate them if she wanted to. By changing her thoughts, she was changing her world. Actions followed thoughts.

We advanced into the unconscious mind, influencing the dream department. My treatment took the following form: 'Imagine you are saturating your long-term memory with white light, focusing on the happy times in your life. Now, enlarge your feelings about these happy times! Remember them as often as you can.

'You are realising that the difficult times in your life were your learning processes and examinations. Once you passed them they become unimportant and out of date, and can now be eliminated.'

'Find a sense of humour in yourself and amplify it. Make it bigger and bigger. See the funny side in almost every situation. Smile and laugh as much as you can!

'Still drawing in the white light with its unconditional love, you are cocooning yourself in that light; you can now feel the unconditional love saturating your body. There is plenty of light to share with someone else.'

I then introduced her future partner. I described him in detail and asked her to visualise him. Still feeling that love in the centre of her chest where the heart chakra is, I asked her to send her image up into the universe. Then I slowly woke her up.

The lady felt uplifted and positive about our experiment and left in a happy frame of mind.

One month passed.

The lady mentioned that so far she had not met anyone.

The second month went by; still no boyfriend.

Slowly the lady became withdrawn again and began staying at home at weekends.

At the beginning of the third month she rang me to say she'd received an invitation to a friend's engagement party and felt she might as well go.

'Definitely' I agreed.

The following Monday the lady rang me excitedly to tell me I was right.

When you love somebody you cannot live without them. She had met her future husband, the brother of the person whose engagement party she went to!

59 Children Have A Need To Understand

James's father used to come to me for treatment regularly for years. He suffered with a slow degenerative illness which had seriously affected his breathing. Each treatment helped him continue working as a scientist for longer than he could have ordinarily have expected to. Eventually he was too ill to continue, and he died.

James's father did not believe in an afterlife, yet towards the end of his life he started reading books about it.

James was eight when his father passed away. He was an only son and very close to both his parents. His mother contacted me a few months later, telling me that James was unhappy and appeared very angry towards his mother. She thought that I might be able to help.

James used to have a massage occasionally, which he always enjoyed. During one particular session we talked about many subjects and eventually mentioned his father. As soon as he gave the go ahead to talk about him, I asked if he'd ever seen him since his death. He admitted he saw him every night standing near his bed.

'But he never speaks to me.' He seemed upset about that.

'I know why he doesn't talk to you,' I replied.

'Why?'

He could hardly wait for the answer.

'Imagine we are a spirit with a body. Imagine our spirit can never die because it is a life force and is eternally young. Now imagine that our body is a kind of vehicle that we use to get around and express ourselves with on earth. Eventually our body gets old or worn out when it's time to leave the earth. The soul or spirit then frees itself from the vehicle that doesn't work anymore. We call that death. As you have seen for yourself, your Dad is very much alive when he comes and stays with you at night. The only thing is he can't talk because a part of his body he has left behind is his voice box.

'On the other side where he is now, people communicate with each other, through a mind to mind conversation called telepathy. I suggest the next time you see your Dad, talk to him in your mind, then leave a gap for his answer which will come to you as a thought.'

James completely understood, and was suddenly very carefree.

At the end of the massage I asked him to close his eyes.

'I am going to tell you a little story. Just close your eyes and listen.

'You have told me that you want to be a pilot one day. Imagine you are in a special aeroplane as a co-pilot. The plane is flying higher and higher. Eventually you are above the clouds. The pilot parks the plane on one of the clouds for you to get out. It is a very fluffy, bouncy cloud, quite large. It is fun to use the cloud as a trampoline. You are jumping higher and higher, somersaulting backwards and forwards. You are feeling so happy.

'Suddenly you realise that you are not on your own. Somebody else is having fun and jumping with you. It is your Dad. He is so pleased to be with you and to do all the acrobatics as well. You are having a wonderful time!

'Eventually you feel like a rest. You are sitting down with your Dad having a chat. Remember… in telepathy. You can ask him anything you want. He will answer. You can tell him everything you always wanted him to know.

'I'll leave you chatting for a little while.'

After a few minutes I continued.

'The pilot is waiting for you. It is time to step into the aeroplane. Slowly the plane descends and lands safely on the ground.

'Before you open your eyes, I just want to tell you that any time you go to sleep and you want to talk to your Dad again, you can repeat this exercise and be a co-pilot again.'

When James opened his eyes, he was smiling. I enquired if he had seen his Dad. 'Yes,' he declared, 'and Granddad too.'

I was glad to help him in such a spiritual way.

James was much happier when he left.

60 It Is Never Too Late

A few years ago Miss St. came to me for help. She was in her mid-thirties. She felt deeply hurt, upset and bitter and blamed her mother for everything that was wrong with her life. She told me she was a top accountant. Everybody thought her very intelligent and good at her work. But she was never good enough for herself, no matter what she achieved.

In her view it was all due to her mother who had died when she was just twelve years old. For as long as she could remember, her mother had always discouraged any attempts she had made to learn or to achieve goals she might set herself.

She resented her mother, blaming her for ruining her life and in particular for her self-hatred and feelings of inadequacy.

She hoped I would be able to do something for her. I pointed out that I couldn't do anything other than perhaps help her to find her own way. She wanted to know how many times she'd have to come for hypnotherapy.

'You need to attend as many sessions as it takes you to forgive your mother for what you think she has done to you.'

'I'll never forgive her.'

Eventually I was able to help her open up to the possibility of forgiving her mother by exploring the behaviour patterns of her grandparents and showing how their repressive anxiety and inability to express affection had been perpetuated through the generations. There was quite a likelihood that she might act similarly with children of her own in the future. From one angle the protectionism could be seen as a form of love, an attempt to save offspring from possible failure.

Miss St. had never looked at her situation in that light before and, a little hesitantly, agreed to meet her mother and ask her for forgiveness under hypnosis.

Miss St. went easily into deep hypnosis. The white light was introduced, with all its positive features such as unconditional love, forgiveness, self-forgiveness, upliftment, physical and mental harmony, self-love and so on.

I suggested, 'You are breathing in unconditional love. It means accepting love without having to give anything in return. You distribute it into your mind, especially into the long term memory. You are feeling the love in the centre of your chest, and from thereon feeling it spread all over your body. You are feeling accepted for what you can and can't do. You are feeling very capable, able to do anything you want to master; viewing your life with self-understanding, self-love and self-acceptance. Feel that love growing inside you. Continue to breathe more and more love into every cell of your brain. You are totally saturated with that love and light. It is completely enhancing your way of thinking, particularly about yourself and others. There is no blame, only love and forgiveness, as well as self-forgiveness.

'With all that love within you and so much to give away, I want you to visualise your mother clearly. As you do it, feel that love increase more and more. Ask your mother to come closer to you, still sending that love to her. Then talk to her and tell her lovingly, what you always wanted to say to her…'

When she came out of hypnosis I asked her for the details of what had happened. She described how her mother had stayed at least forty feet away from her and she had wondered why she didn't want to come nearer. We considered how frightened Miss St.'s mother might have felt at her daughter's anger, when with the enlightenment that comes after death she had finally realised the harm that had been done by her well-intentioned protectionism.

After the following session Miss St. confessed that her mother had finally come close to her. They indeed forgave each other and created between each other the love that had been missing.

After six sessions Miss St. was not only free from the destructive thoughts about herself or blaming somebody else, but her relationship with her partner had picked up significantly. I had not been aware that they had difficulties.

I learned from this case history that it is never too late to make up. There is no barrier between the two worlds. Once again, change your thoughts and you will change your world!

61 Evidence Of Survival

'Forgiveness is the key to Peace'

Edward was a longstanding friend of ours. He lived with his brother, Jim, who was considerably younger than him. Both brothers had lost their wives a number of years ago. Although they were very close, they never really communicated with each other. Both had good jobs before they'd retired. Jim had managed to save a large sum of money, whereas Edward had no savings. He was very good-hearted and had given most of his money to relatives over the years.

One day Jim, who had suffered various heart attacks a few years back, died suddenly from the same complaint. His savings went to the rest of the family. Edward received nothing. Although Edward was not at all money-minded, it hurt him, as he thought his brother had not considered him at all.

Almost immediately after the funeral Edward heard his brother call him. He described it as a voice in his head, clear and loud. He recognised his brother's voice. When he answered him, asking what he wanted, there was always silence. Edward became quite disturbed about this happening. He started worrying about his brother. Also the brother used to disturb his sleep at times.

When Edward told me the story, I suggested that if he really wanted to find out why his brother contacted him so desperately, he should try hypnosis. He immediately agreed.

I soon had him hypnotised.

'You can hear my voice and you can also speak. Can you hear me?'

'Yes.'

'I want you to think of Jim and how much you cared for him. I want you to feel that love in the centre of your chest. Sending that love to your brother, I want you to visualise him as clearly as you can. Can you see him?'

'Yes.'

'Still feeling that love for your brother, I want you to ask your brother why he still calls you.'

To my surprise, Edward asked him out loud. Then he told me the answer.

'Jim said that he is very sorry for not leaving me any money in his will. He always thought that I would die first, as I am older than him.'

'He is now asking for forgiveness. What do you want to say to him, Edward?'

'You shouldn't have been so inconsiderate!'

I reminded Edward that his brother needed his forgiveness. Jim was sorry for what he had done, or rather for what he hadn't done.

'Of course I forgive you, brother!' Edward called out.

Strangely, after the hypnosis, Edward never heard Jim's voice again. He seemed to have found his peace.

The episode raises the question: If we take our spirit or soul with us to the other side, what is the soul? Is it a life force which includes our mind? We have to distinguish between the brain, our physical computer, and the mind which includes both, consciousness and unconsciousness. If we take our mind with us, what is it made of? Do we take our emotions, both positive and negative, and all that is known about us? Jim showed us that guilt can make us quite restless from the other side.

Some of the following case histories may shed more light on this mystery.

62 George's Past Life – 'Out Of The Blue'

George came for a relaxing hypnosis. He had a stressful and demanding job. After the deep tissue massage I gave him, which included a consultation, we started the hypnosis. I suggested going down a safe, secure escalator which would eventually lead into a special room.

'This room is your own private place. It is just for you. You can decorate it the way you want, put a carpet into it, a TV and a hi-fi system. Just make it completely to your liking….'

As George was only twenty-four years old, I was trying to make his special room modern. After the session I asked him if he liked his special room.

'No, I did not!'

He was adamant.

'Why not?'

'I put a TV into the room, as you suggested, that went straight out again. Then a carpet and then a hi-fi… that vanished as well!'

'What was in your room?'

I was curious.

'An old oak desk. The windows were funny-shaped, like those in Hampton Court Palace.'

'You mean Tudor Style?'

'Yes.'

'If that was definitely your room, what profession would you say you had?'

'A doctor.'

'You mean a medical doctor?'

'Yes.'

I carefully explained about past lives and that he might have regressed during the session to such a life, although we were not aiming to do that. As it was completely new to him, I asked whether he would like to investigate it further.

He said he definitely wanted to.

The next session was a past life regression.

It turned out, after some investigation, that he lived under Queen Anne (1665 - 1714, reigning from 1702 - 1714,) in Haslemere as a medical doctor. He was married and had two children. He gave the names of everybody he knew and described the village to me.

It intrigued him so much that he drove to Haslemere, a place he had never heard of before. He was also unaware of Queen Anne's existence. I told him to see the vicar and ask for details of the names he had come up with, telling the vicar that they were his ancestors rather than names from George's past life. Unfortunately he went on a Saturday and the vicarage was closed. As far as I know, he didn't pursue the matter any further.

To me it was real evidence of a past life. He was ignorant of the existence of other lives and he had never heard of Queen Anne before, who had only ruled for twelve years at the time.

63 More Evidence Of Survival

I Had to Come Home

Chris, a 25 year old man, suffered from melanoma. His back had numerous 'bumps' and he told me that he was in considerable pain. He begged me for a deep massage. I had to deny him his request as his condition was a contra-indication. Instead we opted for a healing hypnosis, involving plenty of white light and positive affirmations.

The first session went well. He felt somewhat happier in himself and the pain was less. After the second appointment he had the same, positive reaction. Again he desperately wanted a massage, which I had to deny him once more. He cancelled his third session saying he was starting with chemotherapy the next day, but promised he would be back when the course was finished. Unfortunately he passed away three weeks later.

Six months went by and his sister came for treatment. She explained that she was slightly psychic and had heard her brother talking to her. She asked him why he had to die. He answered, 'I had to come home!'

She came every fortnight from thereon and each time she told me a different story about new things her brother had told her. 'I took my mother to Bournemouth. On the way home my brother Chris said: 'Christa goes there for relaxation. Do you?'

At the time we had a house in the area which we often rented out. I had to keep an eye on it, so I went down there every week. I must have mentioned it to her sometime in the past, that's how she knew about me going there, I told myself.

'Yes, I do go to Bournemouth,' I told her. 'It used to be for relaxation. Now it is more like aggravation.'

The following fortnight she explained to me that her brother had advised her to start packing as they would sell their house very quickly. She then confided that they had been trying to sell for two years and not one person had come to view it. She concluded it was because we were in a recession. Nobody could sell.'

I agreed with her.

The following fortnight she was very excited. 'Guess what! We have to vacate our house in ten days. The Housing Association have bought our house!'

I was stunned and began to believe what her brother had told her.

Another fortnight passed and the lady could not wait to tell me she and her sisters had gone to an artist's colony seaside village. When they left the hotel she heard her brother say, 'One of you will strike it lucky today.'

They went to an antiques and flea market. One of her sisters picked out a particular dirty, ugly looking ring. She asked the price. The lady explained that she was looking after the stall for someone else. '£1.60,' she said, looking at the price tag. The sister bought the ring, which turned out to be a terrific bargain.

I had always liked Chris. I felt that I wanted to tune into him and see whether he had a little message for me. At the end of the massage I suggested to his sister that we both closed our eyes and thought of her brother to see whether we get anything. She agreed and we concentrated on him for a few minutes. I could hardly wait,

'Did you get anything?'

'Yes, but it is a bit stupid,' she said subdued.

'What did he say?'

He said, 'Move over, I want to have a go!'

I had to laugh. He still wanted his massage. It just shows he hadn't lost his sense of humour, even from the other side!

64 Telepathy Or Communication With A Guardian Angel?

'She is on the Way'

Mrs. M., an 80 year old patient, had become one of our best friends. She was a well-known medium in the area. She explained to me how her guide, or guardian angel, helped others with messages. She gave them evidence of survival. Her guide was a young black girl, who she felt must have lived during the era of slavery, as she called her 'lady'.

Mrs. M. worked by appointments only. If people were desperate after a particularly sad circumstance or experience, they turned to her for help. The old lady went into a trance and her guide, would speak to the person in need of help. She never foretold the future, just gave evidence of the person's survival and a message for the loved ones.

The old lady had no transport, so I often used to drive her to her son's in the evenings. I enjoyed that very much. Each time she used to tell me fascinating stories about the afterlife and what she had experienced herself. Mrs. M. was not well read but had great knowledge.

One of those evenings I was meant to fetch Mrs. M. from her son's to take her home. I went as usual to my jogging club first. That particular evening they had a cheese and wine party, starting straight after the run for about half an hour.

To be honest I was already late fetching the old lady. On the way to her son's I thought, if only I could let her know that I was on my way. There were no mobile phones in those days. Then I had an idea. Thinking, nobody could hear it, I said to her guide, 'Tell Mrs. M., I'M ON THE WAY!'

I repeated it twice.

As I arrived at her son's house and rang the bell, the old lady came to the door asking if I had forgotten her. I thought there was no point lying, as she always found out the truth. She went on to tell me she'd asked her guide where Christa was. The guide answered, 'SHE IS ON THE WAY.'

My words exactly!

65 Telepathy Or Electric Shock?

Give her a jolt...

We had just moved into our new house, 25 years ago. Sitting with my husband on the settee we were watching 'Dallas' on TV. It used to finish at ten past nine in the evening. At five past nine I felt a sudden shock go right through me. I flew off the couch with the force of it. My husband looked at me astonished and said, 'What is the matter with you?' I explained that I had experienced a terrific jolt going right through me.

At that moment I remembered the old lady. 'What is the time?'

'Five past nine,' my husband answered.

'Oh dear, I am late again fetching Mrs. M.'

As I arrived at the door a short while later, she said, laughing, 'I asked my guide where you were. When she told me that you had forgotten me, I instructed my guide, 'Give her a jolt!'

I could not believe she had used the exact words I had, describing it to my husband.

66 Amazing

It was a beautiful day in February. The ground was thickly covered with snow and the sun shone brightly. At midday my son, then 13 years old, wanted to buy a pair of shoes for himself. He asked me for the money and I handed him one twenty pound note and a five pound note, plenty of money for shoes in those days.

I carried on working in our clinic until eight o'clock in the evening. As soon as I saw my son I asked him about his shoes. He said he hadn't bought any, so I asked him to return the money. He searched in his coat pockets for it. Over and over again he went through the pockets. The money had vanished. He was devastated.

'You'll have to pay me back with your pocket money,' I insisted.

He was panicking, 'Please mum, let's look for it outside. I was having a snow ball fight outside the house with my friend. I must have lost it there. Otherwise it could be somewhere on the way to my friend's house. He lives three miles away.'

'Do you really think that you stand a chance of finding the money eight hours after losing it? It would stand out on top of the snow. Everybody who walked on the pavements would have seen it during the day, and it is now dark.' I was getting cross with him.

He carried on begging me to go with him and find the money outside. I told myself I could do with the walk. As my son went upstairs to get himself ready for the cold and dark winter evening, I tried to ring Mrs. M., the 80 year old medium who was a patient. There was no answer.

'I will have to try and ask her guide, Topsy, for help myself.'

In my mind I conveyed our plight to Topsy and asked if she could possibly help us find the money somehow.

Mrs. M. often asked her guide, the voice she heard, for help when she lost something. She used to tell me about it afterwards, when she'd found the item.

Still waiting for my son, I slowly went outside into our front garden. From there I turned left onto the pavement which was lit up by a street lamp. I wasn't actually searching for the money, as I had written off the likelihood of finding it.

Suddenly I had this strong prompting to look for it. I looked down and there was the twenty pound note.

I thought, 'Now for the fiver.' A couple of steps forward, there was the money.

I ran inside meeting my son at the door and showed him the money. He stared at me in disbelief and asked where I'd found it. 'Outside, under the street lamp,' I gloated.

We both looked at each other silently, thinking how many people must have walked past the money in the blazing sunshine without seeing it.

67 In A Tunnel Of Doom And Gloom, Stripped Of Belief, Faith And Purpose

About fifteen years ago one of my patients, a medical doctor and his lady friend, invited me to lunch. After an hour's journey I reached their pretty house. It so happened, that over lunch we discussed our views about religion. I am very open-minded and my opinion is that everyone has a right to their own beliefs.

Both my patients belonged to a more modern religious group. I do not want to name it as I feel that the core of every religion is the same: God is love and light – and if you love your neighbour, you cannot go far wrong.

We enjoyed our chat. They had aired their views and I had submitted my understanding of it all. Back at the house, we made ourselves comfortable. The doctor opened his bible and showed me, that everything I suggested was actually evil. One must not contact the dead. Privately I thought, what if they want to contact us? They might want to say that they are fine now, to stop a relative's sadness and worry.

The doctor and his friend expounded their view, they explained to me that the devil will take on the personality of a loved one in order to confuse us. My unexpressed objections surfaced silently. What if the outcome of a message from a loved one helped a person to focus on their life and their happiness again? I couldn't see what was evil about that.

After the bible session we watched a video about some missionaries in the Philippines. I could not believe seeing a totally fanatical woman standing on a stool, her eyes flickering with passion as she delivered her gruesome message. 'And when you have sinned you will go to hell and your flesh will burn to the bone and grow again and burn again, eternally.'

The farmers in the countryside, listening to these words, were horrified. I don't think a loving God would want to frighten us. His commandment was just to love each other. Why is that so difficult?

After the video session we went by car on a half hour journey to the church. When we arrived, the doctor asked me if I had enjoyed the sermon. I said yes but couldn't for the life of me recall one. I concluded that he must have switched on a tape in the car. Somehow my brain must have switched off. I remember inwardly pleading, 'Don't ask me any details, I haven't got a clue what the sermon was about.'

The church was new, big and cheerful. I love churches. They make me feel at home. Although we were late and most seats were taken, ours were empty, VIP, right in front. I wondered why we had been so lucky, or whether it might have been the doctor's standard seat?

In front of us was a large stage with a band playing hymns cheerfully and rhythmically. They had no hymn books. The words were projected onto a large screen. Everybody joined in, singing with their heart and soul. It was lovely to hear. There did not seem an end or a new beginning to a verse. It just continued until about after ten minutes it stopped dead at the end of a line.

Everybody sat down. One person suddenly popped up and talked in tongues. He then sat down and another man stood up and translated what he'd said. I was a bit dubious about the authenticity, but didn't give it any more thought, strange things often happened in my world.

After the service, people gathered on the stage to do healing. I said to the doctor, 'I can do healing, should I join in?'

'No, they pray.'

'I can pray.'

'You have not signed in as a member.'

I thought, 'I'm sure, God won't mind.'

On the way home I had a terrible headache. Twelve hours of listening and being taught must have been too much for me. The next day I felt awful. I had never been depressed before. I gathered that this must be how it feels to be depressed. I did not want to do my work as a therapist anymore. There was no point. All I stood for was evil, they'd told me. Everything I had achieved was suddenly worth nothing. I could not see any purpose in continuing my work. The joy and fun of living had left me. It felt like being suddenly stuck in a dark tunnel.

The following day was just the same. The third day it became unbearable. I had to go shopping. Everything was done automatically. I did not want to talk to anybody. Coming out of the shop I climbed into my car.

'I must get myself out of this doom and gloom!' I said.

Suddenly I felt determined to conquer it.

'I know, I'll sing a hymn,' I said. I chose a particular one which I sang at the top of my voice, while stationary in the car, all three verses of it. As it ended, I felt as if somebody had taken a heavy weight off me. At the same time I realised that I hadn't sung the intended hymn, but another.

'Gracious spirit of thy goodness, hear my anxious prayer, help thy loved ones who are suffering, 'neath thy tender care,. Loving Father hear me…' It is an actual healing hymn, asking God for help.

Who had put it into my mind?

I was my old self again, happy and uplifted.

I knew I had been shown that without my understanding, my spiritual knowledge and the love of helping others, I would have no purpose.

68 My First Attempt

Thank goodness I did not live in the Middle Ages. The thought of it makes me shudder! It seems such a cruel time. Yet the teacher at our hypnotherapy college emphasised that we had all lived before. He even told us how to regress a person into a past live.

I had to know for sure. I had always thought of our teacher as honest and dedicated to his profession. How could he suggest such a thing?

The opportunity to find out arose when a good friend of ours, a 39 year old rugby player, came in for treatment. I asked him whether he would be interested in proving somebody wrong.

Though he questioned even the idea of hypnosis, let alone regression to past lives, he was willing to go along with me. I was open with him about my own scepticism over the issue.

Eric was easy to hypnotise, he was an extravert. In no time he was regressing in time, backwards into the womb and then into a tunnel.

'At the end of the tunnel is a radiant light. You are stepping into that light and are now in your past live.' If there was such a thing, there wouldn't be more than one, I thought.

'You can hear my voice and you can also speak. Can you hear me?'

'Yes.'

Are you in your Past Life?'

'Yes.'

Is your father there?'

'No.'

'Is your mother there?'

'No.'

Have you brothers and sisters?'

'Yes.'

'Are they there?'

'No.'

'Are you on your own?'

'No.'

'Whose is with you?'

'People.'

He then told me, in another long-winded question and answer session, that he had many brothers and sisters, but did not know where they were. He had no friends. As he was a close friend of our family now, I was able to feel his loneliness. Reluctantly he told me about his job.

'Buying and Selling.'

'Where do you get the things you sell?'

'Don't know.'

I felt they were stolen. When I asked him which King or Queen was reigning; he told me there wasn't one. Later when he woke up he remembered more details he had told me under hypnosis. It turned out that Cromwell reigned over England at the time.

I asked him to go to the age of twenty-five. He began to get restless.

'Move on to the age of thirty now. Where are you?'

'Nowhere.'

I gathered that he was dead.

'Go back to the age of twenty-five.' Instantly he started saying, 'Jump, jump…'

I interrupted, 'Jump from what into what?'

'Jump, jump, jump...' he carried on.

As he was not making sense, I urged him to go to a happy time in that life. He went to the age of two. Then I suggested he return to this life, in the here and now. Being aware of his loneliness in the past life, I emphasised how many friends he had here and how much they all loved him, including his family. Love was totally missing in his past life.

As Eric opened his eyes, his first words were, 'Sod that!' He told me that he had committed suicide in his past life. He had tied his ankles together and asked somebody to tie his hands behind his back. Then he had jumped into deep water and he drowned.

'I have always thought the worst way to die must be being trapped under water.'

I suggested he meant drowning.

'No, being trapped under water,' he repeated.

There was also a connection between this life and his past life about having friends. In the past he had had none, whereas in this life, he had so many; it was unusual. He hated being on his own or living alone; friends were never far away when he was studying. He was the owner of a private medical clinic but his hobby was wheeling and dealing. In his garage he kept all kinds of junk, and he knew the market price of each item. His wife would often despair of it all.

When Eric was in his early twenties in this life, he had an accident in which his car overturned. He came out of it unhurt but badly shaken. Apparently he went crazy in the overturned car, or so an onlooker had told him, until he had found a way out. At once I had suggested he was trapped under the water again. It must have appeared to him that way.

It makes me wonder whether we draw accidents to us in this life, to relive the same emotions we experienced in another life, in order to address them and release them.

69 More Evidence Of Past Lives?

Shortly after my first attempt of performing a past life regression, I had another chance to get some more evidence.

A 45 year old man, a good friend of ours, visited us. He was particularly distressed as he had just lost his job. He had suffered from a mild form of depression for quite a while and had been treated by a psychiatrist. He explained that he did not want to take any anti-depressants. The psychiatrist had therefore given him tapes with relaxing music to calm his nerves.

Our friend, Garry, listened to them a few times. He complained, 'As I am listening to the music I don't go deeper into meditation, instead I go deeper into depression.'

I had to laugh and made him understand, 'If the tape had some soothing words as well as the music, you would probably listen to them, instead of your own negative inner thoughts.'

He asked whether I could help. I suggested a relaxing hypnosis with plenty of positive affirmation. I mentally transferred him to a place of his choosing; in his case, a beach. I emphasised that this was a special place where he had never been before, so there would be no memories attached to this scenery.

I introduced, as always, the sunshine, the golden white light in the universe, standing for unconditional love. I described the love and what it stood for: compassion, forgiveness, self-forgiveness, happiness, understanding, confidence... anything you want it to stand for, anything that enhances your body, mind and spirit ...and automatically enhances all mankind ...as we are all connected on a spiritual level by love. Consider it granted.

When he woke up from his hypnosis he looked and evidently felt better and smiled. 'What else do you do with hypnosis?' he asked.

I told him I did past life regressions and was looking for more volunteers. He was very interested and we agreed to have a session the following evening.

After the usual deep hypnotic induction I told Garry he could hear my voice and could also speak himself.

'You are going backwards in time ...you are two years old, one year old, in the womb ...and now you are approaching a tunnel . . you are drawn into the tunnel, it is very safe and secure ...at the end of the tunnel is a light ...you are going through that light and you are now in your past life...

At that point I changed my mind... 'You are now in the most relevant life to this life.'

I was both surprised and satisfied at my sudden change of direction and profound way of thinking. 'Most relevant life to this life,' set me thinking. Is there more than one past life?

'How old are you?' I continued.

'Fifteen.'

'Is your mother there?'

'Yes.'

'Is your father there?'

'No.'

'Where is he?'

'He died.'

'Is there a King or Queen reigning?'

'Yes, King Charles II.'

'What are you doing for a living?'

'I am ploughing behind a horse.'

'That sounds nice.'

'No, it's not.'

'Why not?'

'It's hard work.'

He didn't like hard work in this life, either, I considered.

'I want you to go to the age of eighteen. Have you a girlfriend?'

'No.'

I could tell by his voice that he was getting cross with me.

'I want you to go to the age of twenty.'

He instantly burst out crying, sobbing uncontrollably.

I remembered my teacher saying, 'When you reach an awkward or difficult time in the person's life, tell them that it is not important and to go to a happier time.'

I had to shout to get through to him, he was sobbing so loudly. The pillow he lay on was completely wet.

'Why are you crying? Tell me, why you are crying? Tell me now!'

'My mother, she died,' he called out in desperation.

I certainly couldn't say, 'It is not important,' as the teacher had suggested in my class. Brainstorming, I told myself quickly to say something soothing, yet believable.

'Your mother is out of pain now. She is fine where she is, so there is no need to cry.'

He did not take any notice.

'Your mother is fine where she is now, so there is no need to cry.' I became more forceful, 'Go to a happier time in your life.'

No response, just more sobbing.

I said, 'Go to a happier time in your life, now!'

He stopped crying. His breathing changed to a complete calm.

'How old are you?'

'Five.'

At that point I saw a winter landscape in my mind.

'Is it winter?'

'Yes.'

I thought I'd put that into his mind. I told myself off for it.

He continued on his own. 'It is snowing outside.'

'That sounds nice,' I encouraged him.

'No, it's not.'

'Why not?'

'It's cold outside.'

'Put your gloves on.'

'I haven't got any.' He became upset.

I was hoping he wouldn't start crying again. I had to think of something positive.

'There is a warm fire inside and you are sitting right beside it. You are feeling the warmth going right through your body.'

'Yes.'

Thank goodness for that, I thought.

'You are feeling so cosy and safe now. You are feeling happy.'

At this point I asked him to come back into his present life and slowly brought him back.

As he opened his eyes he was quite disturbed about various aspects of what he had observed. Formerly he had not remotely believed in past lives; now he realised how real they were.

Secondly he made it clear to me that his mother in that life looked facially similar to his mother now; although her body was short and rounded in the past life, it was quite the opposite now.

He also remarked on how desperately sad he felt when his mother died when he was 20 in his past life, and how similarly he had felt when his father died when he was 20 in this life. He went on to explain.

'When you said… go to your past life… I saw Queen Victoria. When you corrected yourself, 'Go to your 'relevant past life to this life', I saw King Charles II.'

That to me meant that we have at least two lives. I now know that there are many more. It also made me understand that we bring certain Karma, usually negative emotions connected with negative experiences, from more than one life into our life here and now, in order to overcome these negative emotions. This can be done in various ways: either through suffering the same fate we had once put somebody else through, or ideally freeing ourselves from our own negative attitude by gaining understanding, self-awareness and other qualities.

I was sure about one thing, though: I needed more volunteers.

Throughout the following three months I hypnotised one person per evening, apart from the weekend. About sixty non-paying friends and strangers, as word got around, were regressed into past lives. Some had more significant outcomes than others. Those people who mentioned monarchs they had never heard of before, or described 'Tudor style' windows and furniture and had no idea about the style, taught me the most, although they were as amazed as I was by some of the results.

70 How Past Life Therapy Can Mend Our Hang Ups In This Life

More volunteers, and stage hypnotist versus hypnotherapist

Mike, the stage hypnotist, was the attraction of a rugby club's special evening. As I had never watched a hypnotist perform live on stage, I was quite excited by the opportunity. The idea of putting people into a trance in a noisy atmosphere sounded like quite a challenge.

Sitting right in front, I felt the surge of energy in the hypnotist as he started. His eyes became alive, almost fiery. It was a powerful performance. He totally succeeded at what he set out to achieve.

Mike was a lively, humorous and quick-witted fellow and we soon became friends. He was very interested in my past life sessions as well.

Mike was easily induced into deep relaxation, as he was an extravert. I used the usual routine, counting backwards in years and then asking him to go through the tunnel into the light, which would represent his past life.

Then I started asking him questions:

'Are you a boy or girl?'

'A boy.'

'How old are you?'

'Twenty.'

Where are you?'

'In Prussia.'

At this point I did not take him seriously, because he knew that I was German, and Prussia used to be part of Germany. I carried on, joking.

'So you are German, so you may as well answer in German.'

With a big frown on his face, he was trying hard to obey me but did not get a word out.

I continued, 'Go one year ahead, where are you now?'

'Strasbourg.'

'So you are French now? You might as well answer me in French,' I mocked. 'What are you doing in Strassbourg?'

'I am a soldier under Napoleon.' The answer came in fluent native French. My school French was not adequate to understand every word. I suggested answering in English but he was not interested.

At this point I need to explain that before the session started, Mike confided in me why he hadn't had a girl friend for the past few years. Apparently he had met somebody once when he was nineteen, he was now about thirty years old; they were close friends until two years later, when his girl friend left him. He was so devastated that he had never bothered with anyone else.

As he was self-employed and most of his business was carried on over the phone, I suggested, 'You are expecting your telephone to ring. You know it will ring. More and more people want your services. In fact the phone hardly stops ringing, you are so popular...'

In the meantime Mike was still in deep hypnosis on my treatment couch. As his French was fluent and natural when he told me about being a soldier under Bonaparte and his girlfriend at the time, I obviously missed various details. Even when I asked him to speak in English, he ignored me.

Suddenly he became anxious. I understood that his girlfriend had left him. He found himself in a forest about to commit suicide.

At this point he willed himself out of his trance. He opened his eyes. After going to the bathroom he just left. There was nothing I could do to make him stay. He assured me that he was fine.

The following morning he phoned me. He explained that to his utter dismay, that evening after the hypnosis, that his former English girl friend had rung him out of the blue. They had not been in contact for about ten years. She was now married and lived in another part of the country. Apparently they had a long chat and remained friends.

From then on he was able to find other girlfriends without the fear of them leaving him. Mike understood that there were strong emotional connections with the girl leaving him in the past life and again in this life; especially as he had taken his own life in the past.

It is also interesting to see the outcome of me trying to boost Mike's business; instead the call from his girl friend of ten years ago was so powerful and personal, it influenced the rest of his live.

Maybe meeting Mike was not accidental either... Maybe it was meant, to make a difference to his life!

71 'Nail In The Coffin – Nail In The Eye'

More evidence of past life karma?

Doris, a friend of a friend, was very interested to volunteer for past life regression. She was a friendly and placid housewife. Her pride and joy was her two year old son.

Doris explained before the hypnotic session that she wore glasses as well as contact lenses for protection. 'Why for protection?' I asked. Then she told me her story.

'When I was about five years old or even younger, my mother told me this and I partly remember it. I was very frightened of people in wheelchairs, people walking on crutches or people who were just ill. If they then also had black hair, I would scream and my Mum had to cross the road immediately, to calm me down. We had no idea why this happened or what it was connected with.

'When I was nine years old, I fell badly and hit my head on a wooden board. The board had a prominent nail, which pierced my left eye. Since then I have been nearly blind there. That's why I am so paranoid about eye protection.'

At the start of the hypnosis I suggested Doris might take off her glasses.

It seemed obvious and natural to do that, as she had to close her eyes anyway. She reacted strongly, becoming petrified, and insisted that the glasses had to stay on. I agreed.

After performing the usual induction, then using the routine of counting backwards in years, I asked her to go directly through the tunnel. At the exit of the tunnel was, as always, a beautiful white light, representing her past life.

'Where are you?' I enquired.

Doris told me that she was in a forest. Her parents had a little cottage there and her father worked as a woodcutter locally.

'How old are you?' I enquired.

'Five.'

'What are you doing?'

'I am worried.'

'Why?'

'I can see my sister.'

'What does your sister look like? Can you describe her?'

'She has got black hair.'

'How old is she?'

'Three.'

'She is lying in a wooden box.'

She continued, 'I am not allowed in that room. The door is shut, but I can see through a little gap what's inside the room.'

'What else do you see?'

'My dad is looking at my sister. Now he is putting a lid on the box and hammering nails into the lid to keep it shut.'

'I wanted to scream, 'Don't do that! She will die!'

'But I could not get a word out, I was so scared. I was not supposed to see that.'

'What happened then?'

'I ran away into the woods. I ran and ran... When I returned I knew I must not tell anybody about this. I was not supposed to go anywhere near that room. I would get punished.'

I was curious: Doris' phobia about her eyes… I wanted to know.

'What has the story about your sister and the wooden box to do with your eyesight?'

She replied, 'Nail in the coffin, nail in the eye!'

I did not quite understand. Did she really believe her eyes, especially her left eye with which she'd managed to see through the crack in the door, were guilty of seeing something terrifying? And if she had managed to intervene, did she think she would have been able to save her sister, who was obviously being prepared for her funeral?

It is almost unbelievable. Do we in some unconscious way blame our body parts for our mistakes and punish them?

The next story also seems to confirm that.

72 Freeing Ourselves From Self- Punishment

Is the profession in our past life related to the one in this life?

Mrs. L. was a kind-hearted married lady with four children. She adored her family. Most of the time she appeared happy-go-lucky and she enjoyed her job, looking after special needs children, immensely. Occasionally she came for physical treatment for a bad back. In fact most of her family used to visit us for one reason or another.

Mrs. L's husband had gone away fishing with the three oldest children, for a week. It was when he returned from there that she phoned me.

She sounded very worried, her youngest daughter an eight year old, had lots of scars and scratches on her face. 'She looks terrible. They will never fade,' she maintained. She volunteered that she had taken her daughter to her medical doctor that morning. He just would not believe her and told her that there was nothing wrong with the child.

'But it is so obvious, she is scarred for life!'

I asked if the girl had had an accident but she insisted the scratches and scars had appeared overnight.

Since I could not get any sensible answer from her, I asked her to see me the following day with her daughter. They both arrived and it was plain to see, there was absolutely nothing wrong with the child's face. She looked as pretty as a picture.

I had to talk to the little girl privately, for fear that these assertions should damage her mentally. I explained that her mummy was not very well and she was seeing things. It would only be for a little while. Then she would be fine again. I let the little girl look into my mirror to show her that she looked lovely.

Mrs. L. then explained to me that she had had the same experience some years ago, and at the time she had ended up in a mental hospital. As she had refused to take any medication from the hospital then, she was discharged soon after she was admitted. There was nothing they could do other than offer her the medication. She apparently had stopped going to work at that time as well. She dressed late in the day and basically let herself go, so she said.

One morning, after all this had happened, her washing machine had stopped working. The engineer visited her. Apparently he took one look at her and told her not to let herself go but to pull herself together. 'There is nothing wrong with you!' he said. It did the trick. She recovered. Whether this engineer was psychic or not, I don't know.

This time, Mrs. L. had been given an appointment with a psychiatrist via her GP about the second occurrence of her seeing the scars on her child's face. She told the psychiatric nurse that she saw me for physical therapy and psychotherapy, and that she had suffered the same symptoms before.

The nurse rang me and asked how she had got better previously and had remained symptom free all these years? I could not help joking that the plumber did it! She must have thought, I was mad, but it was the truth, after all.

This time when everybody gave up on Mrs. L., she had turned up at our clinic again. She had rung me various times before, always telling me the same story about how awful her daughter's scars looked. They were getting worse by the minute, she complained.

Mrs. L. also mentioned her fear of big dogs. One had jumped up at her once when she was heavily pregnant. That would frighten anyone, though, I thought. I also found out that the first time she had suffered these hallucinations, her new neighbour had just moved in. That's why she could remember it so well.

She explained the circumstances of the second episode, 'My husband had gone away the day before, fishing. The following day my neighbour, the same lady who moved next door when my first episode of seeing scars occurred, came to see me. She told me about her daughter's dreadful accident and how disfigured her face was. The neighbour described it in such details, that I felt more and more scared. The next day I saw those nasty scars on my own little daughter's face.'

After trying hypno- and psychotherapy in general with her, I opted for a past life regression. I explained how it would work and the idea behind it, namely that another life or other lives are probably connected somehow with our present life. She was willing to try anything except drugs. She had never heard of past life therapy and was quite dubious, yet ready to try.

When entering the light representing her past life at the end of the tunnel, she found herself in Hampstead, North London. Only it looked completely different as it was hundreds of years ago. She filled in many aspects of the hypnosis at the end of the session as she remembered and retained everything in great detail.

She was about twenty years old and worked as a nanny in a huge house.

One could call it a stately home. The house was surrounded with a huge lawn or meadow; fringed by woods. In the woods lived amongst other animals, wolves or wild dogs which were extremely dangerous. Local people were very aware of the risk of entering the woods.

Mrs. L. was married in that past life but had no children. She lived at the end of a nearby village.

On a particular day in that life the weather was beautiful and the children she looked after, a boy and a girl of about five and seven years old, ran out of the house to play. Mrs. L., their nanny in that life, had a few things to do before she joined them. These took longer than she thought. When she finally reached the lawn, she could not see the children but hear them scream. She realised that they had gone too far into the woods and that the wild dogs had torn into them in a pack. There was nothing she could do. It was too late. Instead of getting help, she was so terrified she ran away to her own house a few miles away.

During the regression I suggested she visualise the faces of each child.

'They have no faces.'

I realised then that they had probably been half eaten by those starved, wild dogs. A terrible thought. I suggested going forward two days.

'Where are you now?'

'Behind a tree.'

'What are you doing behind a tree?'

'Watching the funeral of the children.'

'Why behind the tree?'

'Because they must not see me.'

'Who must not see you?'

'The people, they blame me for everything.'

'How do you feel?'

'Guilty.'

'Where do you feel your guilt?' I thought it might be in her mind.

'In my legs.'

As she was lying on my treatment couch I was scanning her legs, without touching, for vibrations. I really could feel a lot of activity there. I had learned to do healing by either laying on of hands or just scanning the aura.

'Why in your legs?'

'They ran away.'

'Would you be prepared to forgive your legs, as they ran away in panic and not purposely?'

'Yes.'

'Do you feel the guilt anywhere else?'

'Yes, in my eyes.'

'Why in your eyes?'

'They saw it.'

Again we had to make peace with the eyes.

I could hardly believe how we obviously distribute our negative vibrations and emotions into different areas of our body. Maybe that is why everyone has certain vulnerable organs. Maybe that is why we are prone to specific diseases.

Mrs. L. told me she spent the rest of that past life in the little cottage she shared with her husband. She was petrified of people's judgement towards her. Many years later, when her husband died in that life, she had to venture into the village to buy some food. What she could grow, she grew in her garden, but certain things, even medication she had to buy in the village store.

As she entered the shop hesitantly, the woman grocer went for her, 'How dare you come into my shop after what you have done to those children!' There was more and more abuse to follow until Mrs. L. ran out petrified. That was the first and last time she went shopping in the village. She lasted a few more years and then died.

When Mrs. L. came out of hypnosis I asked her whether the woman grocer in that life looked like anyone she knew now.

'Yes,' she said without hesitation, 'she looks like my neighbour!'

It all began to make sense. When her neighbour had moved next door some years previously, she had experienced her first episode of seeing scratches on her daughter's face. The next episode had happened when her husband was away. It was almost as if the grocer, or next door neighbour in this life, had waited for a vulnerable moment, when her husband was not present, to attack her and punish her for what she had done in her past life. She had described her grown up daughter's accident and injuries in such detail that it took Mrs. L. straight back to that past life.

Consciously the neighbour would not have known that she had made all this happen, but, unconsciously she would have set it all up and waited for the right time to pounce. The motive is to release the anger the grocer still had in her system from that other life.

Mrs. L. also needed to let go of her feeling of guilt. In a way the neighbour had helped her to face it; but to release it was more difficult.

Mrs. L. suffered the self-torture of hanging on to her guilt for a few more months. Then suddenly the neighbour moved away and Mrs. L. recovered. Just an after-thought: Mrs. L. had a phobia of big dogs. No wonder!

Was it fortuitous that Mrs. L. loved working with special needs children, her job now in this life, or had payback time arrived?

73 Can The Reason For Being Overweight Be Found In A Past Life?

Mrs.X. was not actually badly overweight, but it was enough to find herself unattractive. She was short in height with a well-developed top half and midriff. She explained that even at school she always wore a cardigan to divert people's attention away from certain areas.

Nevertheless, Mrs.X. wanted to lose some weight for health reasons. We analysed her diet. I always advise not to calorie-count as it will not be a lasting weight loss. Changing the diet for one better nutritionally balanced would be ideal. As she had a slow metabolism, protein would be her main food source rather than too many slow burning carbohydrates. Sugar, a fast burning carbohydrate, had to be eliminated altogether. They are empty calories with no nutritional value whatsoever.

To help stay with the new diet routine, hypnotherapy was being used for reinforcement of what we had already agreed on.

Within a few weeks Mrs.X. lost a considerable amount of weight, enough to notice. During the hypnosis I asked Mrs.X. to see herself in the mirror, wonderfully slim. When she woke up, she declared, 'Thank goodness you did not call me thin, I can't stand the word thin. It gives me the creeps.' I laughed and thought it strange.

A few weeks later she appeared for her next session. She admitted that she had bought a new dress various sizes smaller and ventured out. Immediately her friends admired her, 'don't you look lovely and slim!'

That very day she went to the larder and ate all the cream cakes she could find. 'I hate it when people pay me a compliment. It means they notice me! I can't stand it!' I suggested a past life regression as she had no idea why she was thinking that way.

Her first past life took us to eighteenth century London. Mrs.X. was a young girl who lived and worked in a pub. She had nowhere else to go and therefore had to bear the advances of her boss, the landlord, and some of the customers. It was a rough place. As she was 'well-developed' in the upper part of her body, she tried to hide her chest by wearing wider clothes.

In the following past life she was a native American Indian. She had found herself in a village where people were very poor and most had starved to death. They were painfully thin. A severe drought had destroyed all the crops, leaving the village people with nothing to eat.

Mrs.X.'s past lives show how our hobbies, fears, dislikes and likes in this life, have a much deeper significance than we realise. Even in her case, being given attention and certain words as 'thin' have a far deeper meaning. It also shows that in a past life we may well not necessarily be from the same country as now. Even our race can change.

74 Compulsive Obsessive Behaviour – A Remainder Of Past Life Experiences?

Lucy, a 21 year old woman was one of the students at our hypnotherapy seminar. A special workshop for past life regression was laid on, mainly as a demonstration for us to watch the teacher and to see how it was done.

Lucy volunteered to be our subject. She lay on the floor and was soon in deep hypnosis. Once she had arrived in a particular past life, the teacher asked her to speak.

'Where are you?'

'In a market place.'

'How old are you?'

'Twelve.'

As she woke up later, she filled in all the gaps in the communication. She remembered everything. The actual regression left her feeling sad about the girl she once was.

She explained that she had no actual home in that life. She had lived in a market place during the Middle Ages. She wore a brown skirt, she said in hypnosis. She later explained that it was the nearest colour to the filthy dirty object she wore which she found in the mud. When the teacher asked her name, she said she didn't know. She later owned up that they had called her 'slut' and she had not wanted to say that in hypnosis, as she was so ashamed.

The following day I had dinner with her at the seminar. I enquired how she felt about being dirty in this life. She exclaimed, 'I have always wondered why I wash my hands continually and never seem to get them clean.'

It just shows that even habitual behaviour often originates from past lives.

75 Obsession With Winning A Race – Another Reason To Be Found In A Past Life

Derek, a 49 year old runner, was another one of my many volunteers for past life regression. He was a friend from our sports club who also occasionally had some physical treatment for his injuries at our clinic.

Derek was a lively man and full of fun. He was proud to be a fast runner. Most of all he was looking forward to reaching fifty. He would then be in a different age group for jogging and would easily beat the others.

Derek suffered from a persistent injury that eventually had to be operated on. He realised that after the operation he most probably could not race anymore. But nothing could get Derek down. Instead of winning himself, he invested in some racing pigeons and let them do it for him!

Derek was soon hypnotised on my treatment couch, as he was an extravert. They are much easier to relax deeply than introverts. Soon he found himself in a town in Devon, England.

'Who is on the throne?' I asked him.

'King George II.'

'How old are you?'

'Five.'

Are you at school yet?'

'Yes.'

'What is your favourite subject?'

'Running.'

'Do you mean, 'sport?'

'No, Running.' As he was saying it he banged his fist continuously on the couch. I watched him, wondering what he was trying to tell me.

'I must win, I must win...' His silent command seemed to come straight from his rhythmically banging fist.

'You are a grown man now, where are you?' I changed the subject.

Almost out of breath, his pulse racing, he gasped,

'I am running.'

'Why?'

'They are chasing me.'

'Who is chasing you?'

'They are trying to catch me and kill me.' He was perspiring with anxiety.

The rest he told me when he woke up. As always, people remember every detail of their hypnosis, if I have asked them to beforehand.

Apparently a witch hunter had declared him to be a witch. Therefore he was being hunted down. The locals had caught up with him and, although he was a very fast runner; unfortunately he was not fast enough to survive. He did not win that race.

They put him on a 'ducking stool'. I did not know what that was. He explained that it is a type of see-saw. You are dipped under water for a length of time. If you drown you were not guilty but if you lived you were. That meant 'burning at a stake.' It was a lose-lose situation.

Derek was easy to hypnotise and entered hypnosis incredibly deeply. It took quite a while to get him out of it.

A few weeks later Derek had the physical operation related to his sports injury. It was a routine operation, yet when he woke up, he found he had five doctors by his bedside. It had taken him seven hours to awaken from his anaesthesia. He told me afterwards that during the anaesthesia he had relived his past life once more, in detail.

Derek was obviously desperate to free himself from negative emotions such as fear for his life and possibly anger at being punished wrongly in his past life. In this life running, or better still winning, was vital for letting go of those emotions.

I found it unusual and significant that Derek had regressed to the same past life twice – once voluntarily and a few months later involuntarily. This could invalidate the attitude, that past lives or for that matter hypnosis itself, are created in the mind from something we may have read or seen on television before.

76 Are Physical Symptoms Connected To Previous Lives?

Paul, a married 40 year old black gentleman. presented to our clinic with back pain. He suffered from extremely tight muscles on both sides of his body. He pointed out that only the right side of his body hurt. The left side, although the muscles were just as badly contracted, merely felt numb. He explained that, as long as he could remember, the entire left side of his body had felt completely numb. Recently he had encountered an incident where part of his hand had been caught in a mangle at work. A workmate had called out to him and only then had he become aware of what was happening. He managed to free his hand in time. When he showed it to me, the hand was still swollen. How frightening such a close shave must have been! Think what might have happened...

Paul had been examined at a well-known hospital for paralysis. They found no evidence of a stroke or other abnormalities in the brain. They could not explain where the numbness had originated from and asked him to return to hospital if his complaint worsened.

At the end of the deep tissue massage, I applied as I often do, a gentle cranial technique. Soon Paul was deeply relaxed. Watching his rapid eye movement, I guessed that he was probably dreaming. When he opened his eyes a few minutes later, I asked him whether he saw, felt or dreamt anything out of the ordinary. Instantly he mentioned a twelve year old black girl, with war paint in her face.

'How did you feel about her?' I was curious to know.

'It sounds ridiculous, but I was scared of her,' he admitted.

'This could be related to your past life,' I said. 'How do you feel about that idea, and do you want to investigate it further via hypnosis?' I asked. He was clearly interested so we made an appointment for a hypnotherapy session to investigate the significance of this girl.

It took three attempts at hypnosis, each failing when I asked Paul to talk. Although he was deeply hypnotised, as soon as he attempted to speak, he brought himself out of hypnosis. There was only one way to continue, using two fingers of the non-dominant hand to answer my questions.

The principle behind this procedure is as follows: the dominant hand is generally connected to the opposite side of the brain: the rational thinking hemisphere. The other, non-dominant, hand is connected with the creative hemisphere of the brain: dancing, singing, poetry, dreams, relaxation, art and colours emanate from that part of the brain. Talking, walking, censorship and the like belong to the rational side. When a person is right handed, the left side of the brain is the rational thinking one and vice versa.

Paul, being right handed, used his left index finger as a yes finger and the middle finger as a no finger. When deeply hypnotised, I explained you lift the appropriate fingers for yes and for no. It worked well. This time Paul stayed deeply hypnotised for well over an hour while I asked him questions.

I counted down slowly from forty, his age now, to the age of one. He was made aware of being in his mother's womb, then of entering a tunnel and going through that tunnel to the other end where there is pure golden white light. The light feels good and inviting. It leads directly to a former life, a life connected with the numbness in your body.

'Can you hear me?' I asked. I needed to know.

He lifted his index finger for yes.

'Would you like to speak instead of using your fingers to answer?'

Again, the index finger answered yes.

'You can now answer my questions while staying deeply relaxed. Can you do that?'

'Yes,' he declared.

'How old are you?'

'Twenty-one.'

'Where are you?'

'In Barbados.'

I wondered whether he was actually in a past life, as he had lived in Barbados earlier in this life.

'What are you doing for a living?'

'I am a fisherman.'

'Do you like that?'

'Yes.'

'You are now twenty-five years old. Tell me what you are doing?'

'I am climbing over rocks to get to the top of the cliffs… I am falling.'

'What's happening now?'

'I am hurt. I cannot move.'

'Can you get up?'

'No. They're carrying me away.'

'What is wrong with you?'

'I am paralysed.'

'How do you feel about that?'

'VERY ANGRY!'

'With whom are you angry?'

'With myself. I should not have climbed up there.'

'Are you angry with anyone else?'

'With God. He should not have let that happen to me.'

'Where do you feel that anger?'

'In the left side of my body.'

'Is that the paralysed side?'

'Yes.'

Time had run out and I woke Paul up. He explained that he had always been worried he might be paralysed one day in this life. I realised that the emotion of anger was very significant. He appeared such an easy-going person, very kind and polite, but I wondered whether anger was an issue in this life for him as well.

We made a further appointment. The paralysis in the former life would be related to a previous life before that. At least that was my theory, otherwise it would not make sense.

Paul's next past life regression took us to a village in Africa. He told me that his village was being attacked by Arabs who wanted to make him and the people in the village, slaves.

We were using finger language again: Index finger for yes and middle finger of the non-dominant hand for no.

Almost immediately I had a strong feeling that Paul had done something out of character. I had a feeling that he had done something bad.

'Have you done anything bad?'

'Yes.'

'Have you killed somebody?'

'Yes.'

'Have you killed more then one?'

'Yes.'

'Have you killed many?'

'Yes.'

As I questioned his answers in my mind, I realised that they did not match his kind and gentle character now. The word possession entered my mind.

'Is there a possession?' I was dubious about such a thing.

'Yes,' answered his finger.

'Am I talking to the possession?'

'Yes.'

'Were you a human being?' I began questioning the entity, at the same time querying what was happening.

'No.'

I asked myself what else there might be.

The word demon came to my mind. I reprimanded myself. I did not believe in that rubbish.

I still asked, 'Is it a demon?'

'Yes,' indicated his index finger.

'Do you like me?' I wondered.

'No.' said the finger.

'If I ask you to leave Paul's body, will you go?'

'No.'

I tried to convince myself there was little point in arguing.

After a few more questions, Paul answered politely again. I then felt that the entity was not in charge anymore.

'Am I talking to Paul?' I enquired.

'Yes,' the finger told me.

After some consideration I decided I could not see us getting any further with the investigation. The whole idea was to find the girl with the war paint and also the cause of Paul's numbness, which could lead to a possible cure.

I asked Paul point blank while he was still hypnotised, 'Will I be able to get you better with hypnosis?'

'Yes.'

'How many sessions? One?'

'Yes,' said the finger.

To be quite sure, I asked, 'Two sessions?'

'No.'

'Three?'

'No.'

I repeated again, 'One session?'

'Yes.'

I woke him up and told him, 'According to you I can get you better in one session, though I can't see it!' I said.

'I want to come more often than that!' he said. How strange. All three of us, Paul in hypnosis, Paul awake, and I, had different opinions.

The following hypnotic session took us to somewhere in Africa. Paul was fourteen years old. He found himself at the top of a hill with the twelve year old black girl whose face was decorated with war paint. He explained that she was the chief's daughter and he was her cousin.

She was sitting on a wall. I asked him, 'Do you like her?'

'No.'

'Why not?'

He talked in this session, 'She teases me.'

'Don't you like that?'

'It makes me angry.' That anger again.

He then explained that she had said something which made him so 'mad' that he had pushed her off the wall.

'What happened?'

'She was paralysed after that fall.'

Now it started making sense. In other past life regressions I came across reasons why people suffered similar handicaps in this life as they had inflicted intentionally or unintentionally on others in a former life. I also knew that Paul had unresolved emotions still connected with that past life. We had to eliminate it.

'Are you sorry about what happened to the girl?'

'Yes.'

I assured Paul that the girl was still with him. 'Visualise her in front of you, close to you. Now ask her in your own words for forgiveness, if that is what you want to do. You can add anything else that would enhance the situation.' I left a little gap for him to communicate mentally with her.

Then, a little while later, I ventured, 'Would you like to forgive yourself for what you caused to happen to that girl?'

'Yes.'

'Are there any other emotions still connected to the incident which hamper your progress in this life?'

'No.'

'Or to put it another way, is there anything standing in the way of getting the feeling back into the left side of your body?'

'No.'

'Does that mean both sides are now identical in the way they feel?'

'Yes.'

I woke him up and said, 'On your own terms, you are better.'

Paul rubbed his left arm, wiggled his shoulder, stroked the skin silently, scratched his arm and scrutinised it. This went on for a few minutes. Then he said, 'What if it comes back?' I smiled and remembered a certain lady, my very first case. When she was better she had asked me the same question. Only at that time it threw me completely and I hesitated to offer an answer. She noticed it and the spell was broken; her phobia returned with a vengeance.

This time I confidently reassured Paul, 'You are coming back in four week's time for the last treatment: it is either a deep tissue massage or a re-enforcing hypnotherapy session – whatever is needed. No problem at all!'

When Paul returned a month later. I asked him how he was.

'I am having pain on both sides of my back due to muscle tightness. Could I have a massage, please.'

Another thought had crossed my mind, 'Paul, that twelve year old black girl, does she by any chance resemble somebody you know in this life?'

He replied swiftly, 'Yes, my little niece. She is three years old. I have many nieces and nephews, but nobody is as close to me as this little girl. I have often wondered why.'

In other past life regressions I had noticed that significant people in this life are often also significant people in other past lives; only their standing as male or female, friend or enemy may change.

It could mean that our life here is like a play with us in the starring role; close relations and friends as well as enemies are the actors in the play which is staged in this world and our situations and circumstances are part of the story of the play. Its moral is part of our spiritual development; helping each other is vital for the evolution of our soul.

Material temptations, the lure of money or temptations of the flesh and the abuse of power, lead to mistakes, which in turn lead to learning the hard way. I suppose these are what give the play its depth.

77 Multiple Sclerosis And Past Life Regression

My aunt collapsed out of the blue at the age of forty. She was diagnosed with MS. She spent the rest of her life in different homes. She had to be wheeled or carried everywhere but never complained about it. I was only four years old when I recall meeting her first. There was an instant connection of love between her and me. Although she had nothing materially to give, while others spoilt me, I felt particularly close to her. My mother told me, that during the war in Germany, Hitler wanted to kill all disabled people; she was on the list too. The local vicar had saved her.

After a further 25 years spent in bed, my aunt came to the end of her life. Her sister, my other aunt, who was not married either, visited her as often as she could, almost daily. Near the end of my aunt's life she went into a coma which lasted a few days. Then suddenly she woke up. She sang a hymn all the way through, loud and clear, with a strong voice. Then she said, 'I have done it!' and passed away. 'Done what?' I wondered when I was 16 years old, and received the news of her death. 'Done what?'

I now know, she had finished the life sentence she had put herself under for something that had happened in another life in which she might have, probably unintentionally, hurt somebody badly; this happens often by being careless. Nevertheless, somebody gets hurt and somebody else needs to forgive themselves for it. It is probably the hardest thing to do, to forgive yourself for something you have done to somebody else.

78 Just About Anything Is Possible!

Peter's Miracle

Peter was a twenty-nine year old chiropractic student. At the time he shared a house with fellow students, one of which was our son. The house was situated not far from the college in a popular seaside town.

Being a fourth year student, he was learning how to manipulate patients in the clinic under supervision. At weekends he earned some extra money working as a security guard in a nightclub.

One Saturday night during a large and unusually vicious melee, he fell on his left upper arm. During the fall he suffered a spiral-comminuted fractured humerus, the bone of the upper arm shattering into multiple fragments, which prevented him from doing any further manipulations.

Doctors tried to save his arm using plates and screws. His arm was in plaster from the elbow to the top of the shoulder. The accident happened in May about fifteen years ago. Two months later he had to report back to the hospital where it was discovered that the carefully constructed fracture repair area had simply fallen apart rather than healed.

The arm was nailed and plated once more and again put into plaster to give it stability and rest at the same time. Again, by September, Peter had to report back to the hospital and it was discovered that the repair had not taken.

For a third time the doctors set it and put it in plaster. A week later Peter was driving his car; he felt something moist penetrating through the bottom of his bandaged arm. The rod in the radial bone had penetrated his skin and the moisture was blood. He took himself to hospital immediately. It was discovered that it had disintegrated again. The situation was desperate. Peter knew that gangrene could set in quite easily.

Again it was reconstructed.

Almost immediately Peter phoned me and asked me for access to our electro magnetic machine which normally speeds up the healing of broken bones by about forty percent. As he told me his case history, I knew without doubt that the magnetic machine could not help him. If a person does not heal himself, at least to a small degree, there is little hope that a machine will do it.

As Peter sounded so desperate and insisted on coming to London, I could not refuse on the spot. Maybe I could do something, even if only make him more comfortable, I reasoned with myself.

When Peter arrived, he looked white with shock. I put him onto the machine as requested. Then he asked me for a past life regression. I did not like the idea. I did not find it relevant and I did not want to upset him any further than he was already. One never knows where past life regressions can take a person.

I had previously attended an in-depth course on past life regressions. It was run by a leading doctor of psychology along with other leading worldwide psychologists, who had written various books on the subject. The books were specialised and written mainly for psychotherapists and hypnotherapists.

This particular psychologist had studied the philosophies of various religions and was also a follower of Jung. He was especially interested in the approach of Zen Buddhists: to go deeper into pain, to connect with it as they believe it will ultimately lead to the origin of the complaint which then directs the person to the answer and possible improvement.

I suggested to Peter that I should make the session a healing hypnosis not a past life regression. I emphasised a constructive and positive approach, which I hoped would leave him uplifted after the session. He agreed.

The induction was quick and soon Peter was deeply relaxed. I was ready to begin with gentle suggestions, when suddenly I experienced a strange feeling inside me. While making uplifting suggestions to Peter, I was feeling more and more aggravated.

What was the matter with me? Something was telling me to do a past life regression. I felt strongly I had to make him connect with his pain. I could not consciously accept that, so I continued making the uplifting suggestions. My irritation worsened, finally forcing me to give in, but even as I changed my mind, I was worried that I might make his condition worse.

As we began the regression, my aggression subsided completely and instead, many words came to my mind, which I spoke.

'Think of your accident. Re-live your accident. Feel the pain; magnify the pain, get into the pain, own it…'

When he was mentally deeply connected with the pain in his arm I needed some feedback. I asked him if he could hear my voice, and he replied, 'Yes.'

Do you feel or see anything still being connected with the pain?'

'There is a wagon,' he declared.

He explained to me it was a 'covered wagon', the type the early settlers used for travelling across the Old American West.

I continued, 'What is your name?'

'Tom.'

'How old are you?'

'Nine.'

'Have you any brothers or sisters?'

'Yes, one sister.'

'What is her name?'

'Katie.'

'How old is she?'

'Six.'

Then a tear ran down his face.

'Why are you upset?'

'Katie and I had an argument. I pushed Katie off the wagon.'

'What happened?'

'She broke her arm.'

At that moment I did not believe him. I thought that he wanted to make the story fit his broken arm.

'Go forward one year. You are ten years old now.'

Suddenly his face shook with emotion and he looked desperately upset.

'If you want to cry, cry,' I said.

'I don't like to,' he mumbled.

'Why are you so upset?'

'Katie died.'

'How did she die?'

'She fell off the wagon, broke her arm, had a fever and she died.'

I realised that the break might have been complicated and there would have been no medical doctor to set it. Gangrene must have set in and Katie would have died of blood poisoning.

Inside me the aggression restarted. When I spoke it was with authority.

'Now you want to exchange your feeling of guilt for your arm… It does not work that way! I want you to look at the situation with adult eyes. Two children were arguing. One pushed the other off the wagon. It could have been the other way around, she could have pushed you. The whole thing was just an accident.'

I realised that Peter was still blaming himself for Katie's death. He needed her forgiveness.

'Do you love Katie?'

'Yes.'

'Does she love you?'

'Yes.'

'She has long forgiven you if there is anything to forgive. But if you want to make up for it, you have chosen the right profession. You can help thousands of people in your lifetime.

'So, stop cutting yourself off from your arm. Stop withdrawing from your arm. Put the love back into your arm. Put the life force back into your arm. Tell it to heal now, you've got no time to lose!'

My aggression had gone. My brain seemed empty. I asked Peter to wake up.

He opened his eyes and said, more to himself than to me, 'That wagon was so real!'

After a short while, a thought came to my mind.

'Did Katie have long or short hair?'

'Beautiful golden blonde long hair,' he answered, rapt.

'What about your girlfriends in this life… short or long hair?'

'All long hair.'

'They are not Katie,' I explained. 'They are all different people. Katie is with you on the Love Vibration anyway.'

Peter had a little snack and returned home.

A week and a half passed. My husband and I went to the house where Peter lived, to visit. When we entered the kitchen, Peter stood there chopping onions for his lunch. He had his back towards us. He looked strangely mobile. He wore a long sleeved white shirt.

'How is your arm?'

'I am going back to college on Monday.'

'What about your plaster?'

'That came off a week after I saw you.'

Peter had not told me that he had to attend the hospital a week after seeing me; they wanted to keep a close eye on him.

He pulled his sleeve up. There was no plaster. I looked closely at the scar. It was pink, not red, as if it had healed a long time ago.

What do you do when you see a miracle?

We were all silent. Peter carried on chopping the onions. I left the room to collect things from next door. Then my husband and I took off home again by car.

About an hour later I found my voice again.

'Do you think that Peter credited the electro-magnetic machine with having done a good job?'

My husband replied, 'I asked Peter that when you left the room.' He told me, 'No, it's what your wife did, last time I saw her.'

The strange thing is that it was all done against my will and I could never repeat it again. I learned something from that session which I had never realised before. We can heal ourselves by sending Love, our Life Force and Healing into areas of our body which previously have been neglected for negative reasons.

Why do we have vulnerable body parts? Is there a reason for everything that happens? And does even the choice of our profession, or our hobbies, have a deeper meaning?

79 Caren's Cystic Fibrosis – Is There A Reason For Everything?

Caren, a close friend of our family, visited us for a few weeks from Ireland. She had been diagnosed with cystic fibrosis from the age of eight. We suggested physiotherapy, as well as pulsed electro-magnetic treatment. She responded well and had several sessions per week, as she was only here for a month.

I also introduced hypnotherapy, in particular what I call a healing hypnosis, with plenty of positive suggestions as well the use of colours, like blue and gold, standing for healing and unconditional love.

After the first hypnotic session, which wasn't a regression, she opened her eyes in astonishment. 'That was strange… I was a black woman with a black baby in my arms!' I wondered whether it linked to a previous life.'

'Would you like to investigate it further?' I asked.

'Yes, I would.'

During the next session I asked her to reconnect with seeing herself as a black lady. As she talked to me she explained that she lived in a mud hut in Africa with her toddler. I enquired whether she had a husband.

'It doesn't matter about a husband,' she declared.

'What are you doing?'

'I am helping to put out the fires at the opposite end of the village.'

'What fires are they?'

'The witchdoctor from the other village is attacking our village and trying to burn it down.'

'Why?'

'The witchdoctor is after me, to kill me.'

'Why does he want to do that?'

She did not answer me. She had to rush to her own hut. It was on fire! The baby was crying inside. Within seconds the hut was engulfed in flames, too fierce for anyone to rescue the child. Then there was silence. The child was dead.

Caren desperately tried to get into the hut but was held firmly back by two men. They knew that if she went into the hut, she too would die. In a terrible state, the two strangers took her into the jungle.

'Why did they do that?'

'They were hiding me. The witchdoctor was trying to kill me.'

'Why would he want to do that?'

I did not get an answer. I asked for more information about the two men who helped her hide.

'Were they from your village?'

'No. They were white.'

'What were two white men doing there?'

'They were explorers.'

'Do you know these two men in your current life?'

'Yes.'

'Who are they?'

'They are my husband and my granddad.'

Although I knew that she was close to these men in her life now, I was still amazed by the answer.

'Does the baby remind you of anyone in this present life?'

'Yes. My sister.'

Things began to make sense to me.

During the third session I focused on finding out more about why the witchdoctor had wanted to kill her.

'You are deeply relaxed and you can also speak... I want you to go back to an early time in that same life. How old are you?'

'Three.'

'Have you got a mother?'

'My mother died.'

'Who is looking after you?'

'The medicine man of the village.'

'What is your religion?'

'Hindu.'

'Who do you pray to?'

'The volcano.'

It did not make sense.

She agreed with me later, when she woke up, that it was a strange story. I gathered at that point that the villagers prayed to the volcano and that Hinduism as a religion had been introduced by the immigrating railroad workers.

It was just a thought.

I continued the questioning.

'You are twelve years old now. What are you doing?'

'The medicine man is teaching me to heal with bones. He helps sick people.'

'You are twenty years old now. What is happening?'

'The medicine man has died. The witchdoctor from the neighbouring village wants to have power over our village. He is bad... he uses black magic. I can do the healing of people but I am not allowed,' she added.

'Why not?'

'Because I am a woman.'

'I can only heal children.'

'How do you feel about that restriction?'

'Very angry!'

'Where do you feel that anger in your body?'

'In my left lung, the one that is worse affected.'

At that point I ended the hypnotic session.

Afterwards I had quite a few questions ready for her.

I remembered that her six year old younger sister in this life, suffered from severe asthma. Particularly during the night when it was dark, her attacks would start. She always asked for her mother. When I visited them once and saw to her at the start of an asthma attack during the night, she insisted on her mother coming. It began to make sense now.

'At what age did your sister's asthma start?'

'As a toddler.'

I remembered that Caren was very protective over her little sister. She actually 'mothered' her. The two sisters were indeed very close.

I pointed out to Caren, 'In this life the symptoms of your cystic fibrosis started at the same time as your sister's asthma, when you were eight and she was about two. In her previous life your sister, then your baby, was a similar age when she died of smoke inhalation.'

'Now that your sister is grown up, does she by any chance suffer from a phobia of darkness or enclosed surroundings?'

Caren was getting excited. 'Yes. Recently she had to run out of a disco. The smoke from the dry ice machine and the confined space suddenly gave her a terrible asthma attack.

Apart from hypnotherapy, Caren had independently received spiritual healing from Charlie, our friend.

The fourth hypnotherapy session was focused on clarifying a few points. I wanted to know whether we could attempt to assuage Caren's cystic fibrosis. I did not want to ask her under deep hypnosis whether she would recover or not, in case the answer was a 'No'.

I suggested to Caren, 'I want you to connect with your black baby in your past life. Are there any emotions still inside your body relating to the tragic accident when your baby died?'

'Yes.'

'What emotions are they?'

'I feel guilty. I should not have left her on her own.'

'You were trying to help others to put out the fire in their huts. Your end of the village was not under attack at that time. You did not neglect her. Do you understand that?'

'Yes.'

'Are you ready to forgive yourself for what you are blaming yourself for?'

'It is hard.'

'Why do you want to punish yourself now for something which was an accident, one too that happened in another life. You have your child, now your sister here with you in this present life. Do you want to punish yourself by making yourself more ill? Do you want to leave your baby alone again in this world?'

'No.'

'Then start getting better. Forgive yourself and appreciate what you have now, a beautiful sister!'

The question I wanted to ask more than anything, was, could I cure her through hypnosis. I thought, if she said 'no', it would only mean that 'I' couldn't manage it, not that she would never get better. I could hold back no more.

Her answer was 'Yes.'

'How long will it take?'

'Six months.'

When I woke her up, she added, I did not just mean with hypnotherapy, with Charlie's healing as well.'

Caren improved - up to a point. She has two children now. Unfortunately she had to return to Ireland and we didn't continue with any further treatment. Maybe it would have worked.

It would also have been interesting to hypnotise her sister to see whether it would have taken her too back to that same life in a mud hut.

80 Barbara's 'Not So Ordinary' Knee Pain

Barbara suffered from severe knee pain for a long time. She consulted osteopaths, chiropractors and even had an exploratory operation in the USA. Nobody could find anything abnormal about the knee. It was a puzzle. My husband, who treated her, recognized that the pain was possibly psychosomatic. He referred Barbara to me.

During the usual first treatment, a deep tissue massage, I took her case history. The massage did not make any difference to the pain she felt in her knee.

Barbara explained that the knee problem had started three months after a car accident she had had, sixteen years previously. To judge from her detailed information it could not really have been related to the car accident because if it had, she would have suffered knee pain immediately.

As there was no other lead to start from, I hypnotised Barbara to relive the accident. She had mentioned beforehand that a relative was driving the car and that two girlfriends were sitting next to her in the back. As Barbara was a slightly bigger girl than the others and they seemed quite squashed on the back seat, she had suggested Sarah, who was sitting next to the driver, swap with her. Sarah agreed and the three slimmer girls sat next to each other in the back, while Barbara ended up sitting next to the driver.

They were driving on the motorway, in the middle lane, at about seventy miles per hour. Suddenly the bonnet opened. The driver of their car tried to manoeuvre it into the left lane to safety. As he could not see anything in front he collided with another car and they had a major accident in which Sarah died.

Barbara was still on my couch in deep hypnosis. I asked her to describe details of the accident. She told me that Sarah, who had sat in the back of the car, was indeed, 'lifeless'.

When Barbara woke up she complained about unbearable hip pain on the same side as her knee problem. She was almost crying, 'It hasn't hurt for sixteen years and now it's started again!'

'Why did your hip hurt sixteen years ago after the accident?' I asked.

'I had broken my hip and was in plaster for three months. They raised my leg and my knee was in a bent position for that time.'

It all made sense now.

'When they took your hip out of the plaster, your knee was taken out of the twisted position it had had to be in, in order to allow the hip to heal. It means that not moving the knee for that length of time and being in an awkward bent position possibly strained the ligaments. There could also be a certain amount of shock and emotion still in the knee from the accident itself.

Barbara's hip pain while coming out of the hypnosis lasted about three minutes and then subsided completely. I made another appointment for hypnotherapy for a few days later and asked her to phone me if there were any after effects.

The following day she rang and told me that she felt sick and angry. I suggested waiting another day. She rang again and explained that the sickness had disappeared but complained, 'I am very angry!'

When she turned up for the following session she was almost obstinate with aggression. 'I don't think hypnosis can help me!'

I retorted, 'I think that you did not tell me everything about the accident.' I felt there was something missing.

'I told you everything I know!' She became impatient.

'Let's see.'

I hypnotised her deeply.

'You car accident has just happened. Describe the scene to me in detail.'

'I can't see anything.'

'Why not?'

'It's all black.'

I realised that she must have been unconscious at the time and re-lived it again at this moment. Believing that we are a spirit with a body and a mind, I suggested, 'Slip out of your body and walk around. Now tell me what you see.'

'The car is on fire!'

She was very upset about it. I felt it important for her to connect with the fire.

'Look deeply into the fire. Where does it take you?'

There was a moment of silence. Then she said, 'There is a house.' I realised that she was now talking about a house in another life, but that it was somehow relevant to this life and the accident.

'Whose house is it?'

'I don't know.'

'Go into that house.'

Suddenly she shouted out in a moment of realisation, 'It's my house.'

'Are you married?' She wasn't in this life.

'Yes.'

'Is your husband there?'

'No.'

'Where is he?'

'He died in the Boar War.'

'Have you got children?'

'Yes, two. A boy of one and a girl of three.'

'That's nice,' I said.

She continued, 'I am cooking.'

Suddenly she had a feeling of urgency about her, 'I have to go out.'

'All right, you are going out.'

I waited a moment and told her that she was now coming back to the house.

'She screamed, 'It's all gone, it's all gone.'

'What's gone?'

'The house is on fire. It's all gone!'

I realised that her children must have played with the fire from the stove and set the house on fire, the cause of their deaths.

'I want you to go one year ahead. Where are you now?'

'In hospital.'

'I want you to go five years forward. Where are you now?'

'Still in hospital.'

I realised then that she must have had a nervous breakdown, after losing her entire family. She would also have blamed herself for the death of the children, so must have ended up in a mental home, ready to die.

'I want you to go to the last day of your life, in that life.'

'How do you feel about dying?'

'I want to die.'

'I know you do.'

'It is now the last minute of your life in that life.' She just breathed out slowly, signalling her death.

Knowing that there is no spiritual death only a physical one, I asked her, 'Where are you?'

'I am above my body.'

'Where is your husband?'

There was a short hesitation, then she called out, 'He is here!' Although she was lying completely still, I could feel her searching mentally for her husband.

'Where are your children?'

Again a short hesitation and the feeling of her searching; then she shouted, 'They are here!'

There was so much excitement and happiness in her voice. It was amazing.

'I want you to connect with this present life now and once more with the car accident. You asked to swap seats with Sarah. Sarah died. You told me that you felt guilty about her dying, as the seat was at first yours. I want you to understand that you asked Sarah whether she wanted to exchange seats. It was Sarah's free choice to sit in your original seat. You also know now that Sarah let you stay in this life while she returned to the other side. One day when you meet again, she will ask you what you have done with your life, the life that she let you live in the physical world.'

'Are you going to tell her that you have been drinking your life away and that you stayed on working in a job you did not like?'

After I woke her up, she was quiet. It was a lot for her to take in. She then remembered that in the previous life in the mental hospital where she had lived after the house burned down, she had sat there all day rocking backwards and forwards.

'After the car accident in this life, I was off work for two years and sat on the sofa all day, rocking backwards and forwards as well!'

A while later I heard that Barbara had changed her job to something she'd always wanted to do. Her knee pain lessened considerably. I have never heard from her since.

81 A 'Possession' Separates From Its Victim And Why

A father had two sons. The eldest son had committed suicide by taking drugs. It had happened before I knew the man.

A few years later the father rang me to ask for a hypnotic session for his younger son. He made an appointment straight away as it seemed rather urgent. The father himself drove his young married son to our clinic. He just dropped him off to fetch him an hour later. As he did not mention any details as to why his son was having this hypnotherapy appointment, I gathered that his son would tell me details himself.

Apart from saying hello the son never spoke. I told him the procedure about hypnosis and asked him why he wanted it. He did not really answer me. I decided that using guided affective imagery would get him talking to me. I asked him to lie down and close his eyes. He did as he was told. I then suggested thinking of a meadow, any meadow that came to his mind. 'Tell me if the meadow has long grass or short grass?'

He answered, 'long grass… or short grass.' Thinking that he would get the hang of it in a minute, I continued.

'Are there flowers in the meadow or is the grass dried up?'

'Flowers in the meadow or grass dried up.' It echoed from him. I decided that this was not working and opted for what I call a happy hypnosis, using plenty of white light which I told him would stand for unconditional love.

'Leave your eyes closed and imagine that you are on a quiet but beautiful beach. You are lying on your towel which is placed on the warm sand. You can feel the warmth penetrating through your skin into your body. It makes you more and more relaxed. You are feeling safe and secure and in control of the situation. You can see bushes with coloured flowers at a distance around you. You can smell the clean invigorating air. You are feeling a gentle breeze fanning your face just perfectly and you can hear the sound of the sea. In your mind's eye you are looking into the blue sky. You are connecting with the colour blue, a healing colour. You are drawing the blue colour into your throat area as well as the area in the centre of your eyebrows, the third eye. The healing vibrations are filling your neck and shoulder area and also your brain, which makes you more and more relaxed and balanced. Total balance is total health. You are feeling stronger and stronger, more and more in charge of your body and mind. In your mind's eye you are now focusing on the sunshine in the sky. The sunshine, the golden white light and the warmth from it give you a deep feeling of safety and security, a feeling of belonging. The golden white light with its vibration of unconditional love, the highest vibration there is, penetrates every cell of your body. You are feeling very happy and contented, full of joy and laughter. Your thoughts are becoming very constructive and you know that constructive actions will follow constructive thoughts. You are filled with love and light and you feel that your body, mind and spirit are being enhanced by this unconditional love. You are feeling fit and healthy…'

Eventually, slowly, I woke him up.

So far I had had no reaction from him and wondered what would happen next.

He opened his eyes and said, 'Great Danger!'

'How do you mean?' I wanted to know.

'Evil!'

'Where?' I asked.

'There!' He pointed to the window.

Bemused, I enquired again. 'Where?'

'There!' He pointed to the window again.

'In this room?'

'No.'

'Where?'

He pointed to the window again. 'There!'

'In the garden?' I suggested.

'Yes,' he agreed.

At that moment his father rang the bell, paid me and they left.

Within a few days all the electrical parts of our two cars went wrong. Eventually we had to have a new engine for the main car, which was very costly.

A month later the father rang me again for an appointment for somebody else. I could not resist enquiring why his son was so strange. The father agreed and told me that on the way home his son had been trying to open the car door continuously, trying to get out while his father was driving. The father had a terrible job keeping him in the car.

Like a brainwave I remembered that when we had moved into our house many years before, the clairvoyant old lady (80 years old) told me that there had been a 'canopy of blue', as she called it, over our house for protection. In those days I dismissed it as nonsense. Could it be true? It would then make sense that when a person is possessed, especially by an entity of a nasty nature, that the entity would have to separate itself from its victim, the person it is attached to, before that person entered our house.

I was later told by the father that the young man had taken drugs for many years and suffered from paranoia, hearing voices. This entity then, having to wait in our garden to reunite with the young man after the hypnotic session, in its boredom had started to attack the electrical parts of our cars. What a crazy idea!

When the session was finished, before the young fellow entered his dad's car, he was aware of the spirit waiting for him and trying to attach itself to him again, outside. He called it 'evil' when he came out of hypnosis.

The old lady, who had been a patient many years before, explained how dangerous it is to take drugs. I thought that she was referring to the addiction but she refuted that and went on to explain how when a person is under the influence of drugs or in a drink-induced stupor, their chakras are open and unprotected. This means that any spirit can enter the person's body and use it for whatever they want. Some people therefore become drunks, some are used for sex and some just through taking drugs, become addicts or worse, become murderous. The entity can enjoy these things only through the victim's body as it has no body itself; it is an energy. Not all energy is from a good source. A strange idea, but quite feasible.

A few years later I met the father by chance in a shop. He appeared old and drawn. His posture was that of a broken man. I asked him about his son. His eyes filled with tears He did not have to spell it out. I gathered that the son had also killed himself.

Another few years went by and I met the father in the same shop again. I did not recognise him at first. He caught my eye because his whole being was filled with radiance. He looked totally at peace within himself and smiled while chatting to the cashier. His posture was serene. I never got the chance to talk to him but something special must have happened to him. He seemed to have found the Light. The change in him was almost unreal.

I was glad.

82 Multiple Personalities Or Possession?

Celia, a lady in her mid-thirties, suffered from deep depression. She actually described herself as suicidal. Her appearance was impeccable and she was well spoken; in fact one could class her as a beautiful woman.

Celia's background was not so wholesome: a broken marriage and the children were now being looked after by her husband. She herself lived in a house which was shared by others. Outwardly she appeared happy-go-lucky, but that was deceptive. As an escort she earned large amounts of money, and drove an expensive car. Celia was not shy about admitting that she drank too much at times. She also took drugs and had many partners. During the usual consultation I asked her:

'Do you hear a voice?'

'Yes, three voices.'

'What do they say?'

'They were talking about me.'

'Do you talk to them?'

'No, I listen in.'

She explained further that she actually did not like alcohol, but when she drank one glass of wine, she could not stop drinking until she was so drunk that she did not know what she was doing and had to ask others about her whereabouts.

'The strange thing is that I seem to be completely safe whatever I do when I am paralytic. But I can't recall anything at all.

'I normally detest taking drugs, but when I have been drinking too much I take any drug and end up with any partner – but I do get paid for it well.

'I also advertise for partners in a paper.'

'That could be very dangerous,' I warned her.

'No,' she disagreed. 'When I talk to somebody on the phone, I know instantly which person I'll be safe with, and which ones I must not associate with.'

I gathered that as she heard voices, there might be a possession present. These entities would keep her body very safe, so they could use it as long as they wished, for their own gratification. We decided on a hypnotherapy session.

When she was in a deep trance, I suggested the following.

'Imagine that you are sitting on a comfortable chair. Next to you on your right is your guide or your guardian angel. On your other side are seated voices, numbers one, two and three. I am sitting next to them as we form a circle.'

When she woke up, she announced, 'When you mentioned my guardian angel, voice number one, who seems to be the strongest entity and is in charge of the other two spirits, directed his attention to the angel and cried out, 'He is useless".'

I explained, 'You are making him useless. You can exercise your freewill to decide who is in charge and what you want to do with your life, but you are not using it. Therefore the entities are taking advantage of the situation and stepping in, using your body as they please.'

During the following hypnotic session I made some suggestions.

'Imagine your mind is like a cockpit in an aeroplane. You have a control seat and control buttons. Imagine now, that you are sitting firmly on that seat. In front of you there are many buttons, some are overused, some are hardly used and some are brand new. As you look more closely you realise that the buttons for happiness, fun and laughter, peace of mind, joy, unconditional love, direction, harmony and many others are all very new. Other buttons which stand for drinking, drugs, sex, negativity, dislike or hate, anger and guilt are overused.

'I want you now to put a plaster over the overused buttons.

'You have now decided that they are out of use for as long as you want them to be. You are aware that you are exercising your freewill. You are in control. You have positioned yourself in the control seat. If you want to be absent-minded at any time, then you can station your guardian angel in the control seat. Now you can safely gallivant, and when you return you will find everything in order. You are always safe and secure, and always in control of yourself, your life and your happiness.'

Celia was getting much better. The only thing that bothered her now was the need to earn money again.

'I haven't earned any money for two weeks. I must work again.'

Since normal work did not appeal to her, I asked her what she would like to become if money were no object.

'A psychotherapist,' was the prompt reply.

At first I thought it funny, then I realised it was a brilliant idea. She would have insightful information on all cases similar to hers and would know how to handle them.

'If you must continue your line of work then why don't you save and use the money to study psychology?'

That seemed to make sense to her.

83 Are We Always In Control Of Our Body/Mind/Spirit?

Tej, a 25 year old Sikh, presented to our clinic with a phobia of passing out.

It could happen anytime, anywhere. Tej worked as a manager and worried particularly about the likelihood of the extreme anxiety attacks happening whilst dealing with a client.

Tej was extremely easy to hypnotise. Almost automatically, without me asking, he regressed to another life.

'Where are you?'

'In India.'

'How old are you?'

'Nineteen.'

'What is happening around you?'

'Soldiers. There is a curfew. Nobody is allowed out after a certain time in the evening.'

'How do you feel about that?'

'They are not telling me what to do!'

He was very adamant about that.

'Does that mean you went outside in spite of the warning?'

'Yes.'

'What happened?'

He hesitated... then exclaimed, 'I see a fire!'

'What fire is that?'

'It is my funeral pyre.'

I was confused. 'Did somebody kill you?'

'Yes.'

'Who else is present?'

'My wife.'

'You are married?'

'Yes.'

'How old is your wife?'

'Fifteen.'

'Is she watching?'

'No.'

'She has to throw herself on my funeral pyre. That is the law.'

'What is happening now?'

'She is resisting.'

'She doesn't want to. But they still make her!'

A while ago I saw a film about 'sati', an old Hindu law. If the husband dies before his wife, she has to throw herself onto her husband's funeral fire. The law is a few hundred years old and is illegal now.

To ease Tej's physical anxiety we introduced a deep tissue massage. As his anxiety manifested itself in the area of his stomach, his solar plexus, I finished the massage with some healing, and laying on of hands, in that region.

The following session he explained that the 'treatment on his stomach', by which he meant the healing, had helped him most. Since I do not charge for healing and professionally concentrate on physical therapy as well as hypno- and psychotherapy, I asked him whether he would like some healing before we started our official session. The healing would be administered by Charlie, our gardener, who was also a friend of the family. In his seventies, he was an experienced healer and also clairvoyant. Tej agreed.

As it was Saturday, Charlie had been to see us in the morning and left to cycle to the cemetery saying he wouldn't be back until the next day.

I mentioned this to Tej.

'What a pity, Charlie won't be able to do the healing today.'

All the time Tej and I had this conversation, he was looking out of the window, appearing absent-minded and almost uninterested. I therefore decided to change the subject, and was about to start his treatment when Charlie turned up after all. He pushed his bicycle along our pathway.

I was excited, 'What are you doing here? We want you for healing. But you were supposed to be on your way to the cemetery.'

'I was nearly at the cemetery when something told me to come back to your house,' Charlie explained.

Now Tej got excited, 'I did that! I told you in my mind to come here!'

I was amazed. While I thought that Tej was merely bored looking out of the window, he was instead concentrating, willing him to come to our house. Charlie 'heard' his thoughts and obeyed.

Charlie performed the healing on Tej's stomach before I officially started Tej's physical treatment. Tej usually came on Saturdays at lunchtime for his appointment.

One particular Saturday I had treated people continually all morning, so I used the spare half an hour before Tej's arrival, to rest. In no time I was asleep and woke up to the ringing of the door bell.

I opened the door.

Tej's eyes beamed with extraordinary strength. As a result I ended up standing behind the door whilst letting him in. Afterwards I wondered why I had done that.

We entered my surgery and Tej sat opposite me on the couch. Again Tej stared with such force and intensity at me that I lowered my eyes. When I realised that he was actually in charge of the situation and I seemed to be the 'victim', I purposefully strengthened myself and met his eyes with an equal force. He instantly lowered his head.

'What is happening, Tej? Why did your eyes beam at me just now?'

'Have you noticed that as well? They are still burning!' he declared.

I was puzzled. Why is he telling me that his eyes smarted uncomfortably when at the same time he seemed to be the one making it happen?

I started treatment with a deep massage of Tej's arm. At the same time I investigated further.

'What exactly happened when you 'beamed' at me, Tej?'

Looking piercingly into my eyes again, he answered with a much stronger voice, 'I am not Tej.'

'Who are you?'

He gave a name I did not understand.

'Why are you doing this?' I said, demanding an answer.

'I want to see who is stronger, you or I.'

'I don't care!' I exclaimed.

I realised then that Tej had been taken over by an entity which had attached itself to him. I also understood why he was having the phobia about losing consciousness. This spirit was trying to take over his body, to put him into a trance. Tej was quite right, this could happen at any time and anywhere, because he himself did not have any control over it.

I explained this to Tej once he had returned to normal. It made sense to him. We made another appointment for hypnotherapy to consult his guide, guardian angel or inner voice, to see whether this problem could be solved.

The following week, as usual on a Saturday, Tej was due for his hypnotherapy session. Before he arrived, Charlie told me that he was hungry. I left Charlie in the conservatory munching his sandwich.

When Tej arrived, an hour later, I was about to fetch Charlie for the short healing session before Tej's treatment. As I entered the conservatory,

Charlie was fast asleep. A half eaten sandwich lay on the table. He looked as white as a sheet. I thought at first that he was lifeless.

Then I realised he was in such a deep sleep that he actually looked unconscious. He was not in a normal sleeping position either. His arms were spread out in a weird way. Judging that Charlie must have been very tired, I decided he should perform the healing after my treatment.

This time Tej was hypnotised with his eyes open.

'I would like to ask your guide to come through and help us.' Instantly his open eyes, became very soft, almost weak. The voice was gentle, like that of a woman. It seemed that we were consulting a female guide.

'What is the reason for Tej's phobia?'

'We don't know...'

Then, as if his guide was pushed aside, Tej's eyes became very powerful. Something else had taken over and beamed at me. The force that had entered and expressed itself through his eyes answered many of my questions. In fact he started giving me clairvoyance.

After a while, all of a sudden Tej said in a panic, 'I can't get back into my body.'

'Just breathe in slowly and deeply,' I suggested. 'Imagine that you are breathing in a white light. Feel that light advance through your entire body. Now breathe it out through the soles of your feet. This is known as, 'grounding yourself''.

Within minutes he was fine.

I suddenly remembered that Charlie was meant to do the healing on Tej.

As I entered the conservatory to fetch him, Charlie was in the same position as before, fast asleep. I was about to return to Tej when a thought entered my mind, 'Just tell Charlie mentally to wake up.' I thought, it was worth a try. Telepathically I said, 'Charlie, wake up now, wake up.' To my amazement he opened his eyes. He wanted to know what had happened.

'You went fast asleep. You must have been tired.'

'No, you put your hands past my face from behind and everything was dark.'

He looked petrified.

'I didn't come into the conservatory until you were fast asleep,' I contradicted. 'You were on your own.' I enquired as to whether he had had a dream.

'Yes,' Charlie admitted.

'Don't say anything else, just come with me to my treatment room and sit next to Tej.' We went back to the surgery.

'What did you dream about, Charlie?' I asked him.

'Your lot!' Charlie said, looking at Tej. Charlie was a cockney.

'You mean, you dreamed about Indians?' I asked.

'Yes.'

'With or without turbans?'

'With turbans; they were all sitting in a circle on top of a hill.'

Now Tej began to get excited. 'That's it! That's it They all came through me, they are my ancestors!'

I suggested that Tej went to see a medium to sort things out. It was definitely beyond my abilities.

A week later he reported back to me. He had seen a medium who had realised his potential. He was invited to the medium's circle for a psychic sitting. Apparently he was more powerful than any of them and they could not handle him either.

I was due for a holiday. We went to Cornwall for a relaxing time.

I could not get Tej out of my mind. I realised that whatever was with him was also trying to attach itself to me.

I decided I had to end Tej's therapy. He was a wonderful person, very kind, but there were two of him.

Eventually my memory of Tej faded. Then he rang me six months later, just for a chat. Again I did not feel right after our phone call. Charlie had also mentioned that he had not felt well after the healing sessions. In fact, after his 'sleeping session' in the conservatory, every time Tej was due, Charlie was missing. Something unnerved him totally. It was understandable.

I never heard from Tej again.

84 Possession Or Spiritual Guide – Or Would It Be Classed As Schizophrenic?

Emma, a single lady in her mid-thirties, was brought to us by her girlfriend. She was booked for a double session with me, a deep tissue massage, during which I usually do my consultation, and hypnotherapy.

Emma told me that she got very angry at times. She then would hurt herself in temper, such as hitting her fist against the wall.

'Do you hear a voice?'

'Yes.'

'Does the voice say nasty things to you?'

'No,' she answered. 'When I am very angry, the voice tells me to calm down. It is not as bad as you might think.'

'Do you hear a man's or lady's voice?'

'A man's voice.'

'Have you ever talked to him?'

'No. He talks to me.'

'Can you ask him his name?'

'He said, he is a friend.'

'We will call him your guide, is that all right?'

'Yes.'

Then Emma suddenly asked, 'Doesn't everybody hear a voice?'

'No. People don't usually.'

'What do you think it is?' I asked.

'My conscience,' was her prompt answer.

'Your conscience with a male voice, and you are female?'

She did not know what to say to that.

'Can you ask your guide whether I can ask him some questions?'

Her communication with him seemed very quick.

'He said you could.'

'Ask him whether he is an ex-human being.'

'Yes. He is.'

'What was his profession on earth?'

'Professor.'

'Professor of what?'

'Science.'

'What kind of science?'

'He doesn't tell me. He is just smiling.'

'You mean you can 'see' him now.'

'Yes.'

'Can I ask him more questions?'

After mentally consulting him, which again was very quick, she said, 'Yes.'

I continued, 'I think that when we are born, we have a guardian angel or guide to go through this life with us, until we die. My personal belief is that this guide advances 'up the spiritual ladder', as we all do, by helping us passively with guidance. If we decide to commit suicide, let's say at forty, the guide wasted forty years of his spiritual development too. Is that right or wrong?'

'He said, that was right.' Then she added, 'I don't know what you are talking about.'

'Oh dear,' Emma gasped.

'What is the matter?'

She began telling me about herself.

'When I was three, my mother left us. When I was ten, my father died. Then different relatives looked after me. Nobody really wanted me. When I was sixteen I had my first boyfriend. I was so glad to belong to somebody and asked him never to leave me. He left me shortly afterwards.'

I explained that he was far too young for commitment and probably frightened by how intense she had appeared. She agreed.

With subsequent boyfriends it was always the same story. Nobody wanted to commit. That's when she decided to take a girlfriend. She had been with her latest girlfriend for a number of years, and they were thinking of buying a house together.

Emma continued, 'I tried committing suicide and almost succeeded a few years ago.'

'Do you remember anything about it?' I asked.

'Yes, I found myself in a tunnel. At the end of the tunnel was a light and my grandfather gesticulating. I was trying to get to him but he waved his arms and told me to go back, because I had a lot of things to do yet; many, many things.

'Then I woke up and had to face all my misery plus the wires in my nose and throat. It was awful!'

Then Emma confided in me, 'In my office there is a man who likes me. He asked me out.'

'Did you go out with him?'

'Yes.'

'Did you say, 'Don't ever leave me?'

'Yes.'

I explained that in his mid-thirties he would probably be quite happy about her suggestion.

She said that he had liked it.

I explained that she needed to make herself totally self-sufficient, not having to rely on anybody, but being her own person, with her own direction in life.

The hypnotic session went very well, using plenty of golden white light, which stands for unconditional love, making her strong, self-sufficient and full of confidence. The light also represents balance, peace and harmony. It stands for truth and can be trusted totally. Forgiveness is also built in.

I pointed out to her: 'With all the universal unconditional love and light you have now absorbed and surrounded yourself with, you will exercise your birthright as a child of the universe. You will take responsibility for your own actions and thoughts; you are becoming very positive and thereby enhancing yourself in body, mind and spirit.'

She was happy when she left. Later I heard that she had married that man from the office and had one child.

This spiritual story showed me that we can exercise our freewill for better or worse, we can choose life or death. It illustrates how our path on earth can be very stony, full of ups and downs... but we are equipped to overcome these difficulties. We can even turn them into opportunities by changing our attitudes towards them.

Another thought arises. If the voice Emma heard told her nasty things, would it be classed as possession or schizophrenia? If one hears a voice giving uplifting advice, is it classed as a guide, a guardian angel, or our inner voice or conscience?

85 From Heroin Addiction To Unconditional Love

Melissa, a mother of two in her mid-thirties, came to me for a massage. She appeared undernourished and acted like a nervous wreck. As soon as I touched her skin, she cringed in pain.

She told me, she was a heroin addict whose veins had collapsed after nineteen years of injecting. Suffering badly from withdrawal symptoms, she had consulted the hospital immediately. She could not physically tolerate the medication they offered her. Group therapy proved just as unbearable. When she mentioned the pain she was in, they suggested a massage.

As soon as I started, I realised that every slight massage stroke proved a kind of torture for her. She also complained of a deep cold in her body which persisted even in a hot bath. I had not dealt with extreme drug addicts before. There was an option of healing, cranial work and hypnotherapy available which called for a quick decision.

'Lie on your back on my massage couch with your eyes closed.'

I placed my hands either side of her head, taking the weight off it. Using gentle touch-hypnotic techniques, I quietly visualised a white light beaming from the universe onto Melissa. At the same time I also imagined from the centre of my chest, the heart chakra, a feeling of love. I directed this love through my arms and the palms of my hands into her head. I felt a connection of energy. At the same time I asked for mental help for this lady.

'Imagine you are lying on the beach. In your mind's eye you are looking into the sunshine in the sky; imagine it becoming the golden white light in the universe. You know that it stands for unconditional love, lots and lots of it. You are feeling the light balancing and harmonising your way of thinking. You are aware that your thoughts are becoming very constructive. You are instantly feeling the warmth of that Love penetrating all areas of your brain cells making you feel warm and comfortable. This glow spreads through your neck into your chest area. From there it slowly saturates your whole body. Now feel the love connecting with the love you have in the centre of your chest when you think of somebody you love.'

When I woke her up, I did not expect too much from this first attempt.

'How do you feel?'

'In my upper body I am feeling warm, but the rest is still cold.'

'It is working,' I thought.

I was so happy.

Then she added,'I don't know what you mean by love.'

'You love your mother, don't you?'

'No,' was the prompt reply.

'Your father?'

'No.'

'Your children?' There was a short pause.

'No.'

'What about your grandparents?'

'No.'

It seemed unbelievable.

'A dog or cat, or other animal you have ever had?'

'No.' Then she hesitated and said, almost to herself, 'Oh yes. When I was six, I had a dog once. I loved that dog. My father had it put down.'

I soon gathered that the dog must have been old or ill. Melissa had probably decided from that young experience that, when one loves somebody, they will go away and concluded the best thing was to not love anybody.

Melissa told me that she had lived with her partner for about twenty years. He had his own business, and therefore she did not have to go out to work. She also had her own car, and they owned their house.

When she was seventeen, she had had to get married. Her husband was only eighteen. They had a beautiful baby girl. As is often the case, when one marries young, many things went wrong due to a lack of understanding and maturity. Her husband walked out on her after one of their many rows.

It probably reinforced her belief once more, that when one loves somebody, they go away. She made sure that she never saw her husband again and always referred to him when mentioning him to her children, as 'the monster'.

During the twenty years with her next partner, they both took heroin. Despite their drug addiction, she had a baby boy. He and the former little girl were brought up under these conditions.

Melissa had various sessions of hypnosis and deep tissue massage. The physical addiction was reasonably quickly dealt with but the belief in herself was much harder to establish. Eventually she felt and looked much better. I obviously included a balanced diet for her as part of the treatment.

As Melissa commanded more energy and began to look radiant, she tried her first job as a barmaid.

She was extremely attractive now and began to be noticed for her looks. In particular one divorced man had asked her out and had paid her compliments. She told me proudly about him. 'This man is asking me out.'

She acted like a teenager and talked about her new relationship at every session. I became concerned.

'If you go out with this person and your partner, who trusts you totally, finds out about it, you could lose everything, your home, your car… and your partner.'

The children were old enough to leave home anyway by now.

To cut the story short, Melissa did go out with this new boyfriend, her partner did find out and her entire family life was ruined. She ended up without the boyfriend in a bedsit on her own, and they lost their home.

When I met her again, three years later, she confessed, 'They were the most dreadful and hardest years of my entire life. I am still on my own now but I am learning counselling.' She added, 'I now realise that during my years as a heroin addict, my brain, my mind and my emotions were all at a standstill. When I came off the drug, I was still nineteen in my mind, with the emotions of a teenager. In three years I did nineteen years of growing up. I am glad that I took that step, I had to do it.'

It was new to me, that when people take drugs habitually, they are stalling their emotional, spiritual and learning processes. When they stop taking the drugs years later, they will have to pick up where they left off.

It also showed me that we can still be a child, an adult or a parent at any time in our lives if we have missed out on it before.

86 Claustrophobia

A few months later, Melissa phoned me sounding very concerned.

'My daughter suffers from claustrophobia. It started three months ago and she can't leave the house at all now.'

Her daughter was soon on my couch for a hypnotic session.

I used guided effective imagery, asking her to close her eyes. Then I suggested she tell me in detail about a meadow, whether the grass was green, whether it was long or short, with or without flowers, whatever came to her mind. As she talked while imagining the landscape, she automatically went deeper into her hypnotic state. I then changed the landscape to woodland at the edge of the meadow.

'Behind the meadow is dense woodland. Can you see that?'

'Yes,' she agreed.

'Something is moving through the trees. Do you see that as well?'

'Yes.'

'You and I are safely holding hands behind a bush. Whatever is in the woods, it cannot see us,' I reassured her.

'Now it is coming out of the woods.'

'Can you see it?'

'Yes.'

'We are both still behind the bush, very safe. It is coming closer, you can see it clearly now.'

'Yes.'

'What is it?'

'A monster.'

'You mean an animal?'

'No.'

'A man?'

'Yes.'

'Are you frightened of that man?'

'No.'

'Do you know that man?'

'Yes.'

'Who is it?'

'My father!'

I asked her to open her eyes.

'You want to see your father?'

'Yes,' she confessed.

Then she explained. A few months ago she had gone up into her attic and had found a photograph of herself as a baby and her father, holding her.

'He looks like me,' she said proudly.

I wondered how she would find his address.

'My mum has got his address.'

'Then ask her for it.'

She was horrified. 'My mum will be very upset, she always calls him a monster.'

'Can I ask her for the address?'

'Yes, when I am not here.' She was still petrified.

Her mother who was waiting outside in the car came in. Immediately she inquired whether we had found the cause of her daughter's claustrophobia. I nodded. 'But you won't like it.'

'Tell me what it is,' she demanded.

'Your daughter wants to meet her father.'

'Is that all?'

I was amazed at how coldly she'd said that, after her daughter making such a fuss.

'Then give your daughter her real father's address and they can get in contact with each other.'

Suddenly her face blackened.

'I hate him! I hate him!' she shouted out. 'He will take my daughter away from me.'

'How can he? She is 25 years old! You don't own her… nobody does. She is her own person. She can make her own decisions.'

It took another fortnight for Melissa to give her daughter the address.

Her father was over the moon. He too had fretted for his daughter for many years. He too had become claustrophobic because of it. He thought that he had lost his daughter for good, so in his second marriage when he had another daughter, he gave her the same name as his first daughter.

Needless to say, Melissa's daughter was fine after that.

Melissa came to terms with many newly learned experiences.

She is happily retired now.

Conclusion

Life's journey consists of many individual parts which will eventually form a picture. When the picture is completed, that door shuts and another will open. With it, changes occur. We are suddenly uncertain of our future, and worse, we do not feel in control. Often we are about to give up, only to find a sudden breakthrough in our 'impossible' situation. Each step we take is part of a long eventful journey, which does not end in this life, nor does it start at birth.

It is hard to believe that the worse our experiences, the greater the spiritual benefit. As a person we become stronger. The dreaded ups and downs in life teach us the value of positive feelings and emotions and put the importance of material things into perspective.

We have control over our decisions and have certain personal responsibilities to ourselves: to keep our body in good shape by eating the right kind of food and exercising; to think constructively and act on our thoughts in the same way; to welcome new experiences and learn to view difficulties as opportunities.

A lesson not learned will represent itself again and again in our lives until we eliminate the fear of experiencing it, and once this is accomplished we need to let it go. Lingering bitterness about a 'hard done by' situation means failure and could lead to a future repetition.

However lonely we may feel, we are never on our own. During our lifetime on earth our unconscious mind is connected with the white light in the universe or the ultimate intelligence of God. We have access to this universal intelligence and knowledge. Just think how often we connect with it when we are inspired, or when we pray.

Don't doubt the deliverance of your prayer. See it as a letter sealed, stamped and posted. Don't look back. Expect a definite answer from the universe. If your wish is not hindering your spiritual development, there is no reason why it should not be granted. You may have to wait a little if the timing is not quite right; see it as a test of patience and tolerance. All the time you know that it is yours already!

Whatever way you choose: prayer, meditation, self-hypnosis or hypnotherapy, each in turn is equal in power, so long as you intend it to work for you. Remember, we might want something consciously, yet unconsciously we could be scared of that option. Enjoy your life daily. Count your blessings.

Happiness comes from within. One thing is for sure, we cannot build our happiness on somebody else's unhappiness.

We alone are responsible for what we come here to learn. Don't blame anyone else. Remember, we don't know the real picture until we are on the other side, one consciousness again.

Know when you are on the right path and when in doubt, ask yourself. You already know the answer. If it does not feel right, don't do it! We are all children of the universe and have come here to enhance our spiritual development. Just be honest to yourself. The universe stands for ultimate truth, forgiveness and unconditional love.

It is the unconditional part that gives love its magic.

We know that the only currency little children, animals and for that matter plants understand, is love. Many people seek love in power and money – love is too dear to be priced, that's why it is free. So give it away freely, and it will be yours to keep, always.

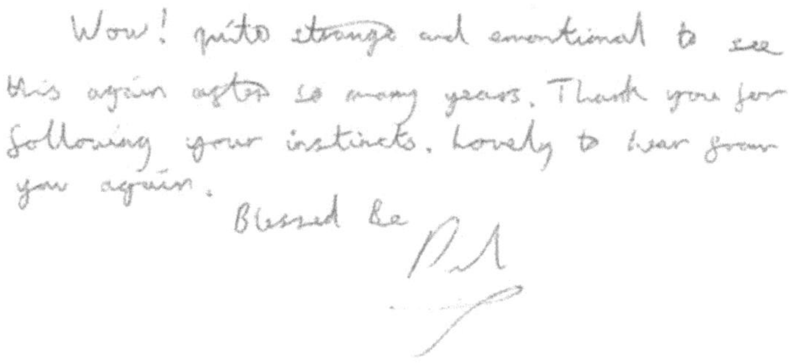
Wow! quite strange and emotional to see this again after so many years. Thank you for following your instincts. Lovely to hear from you again.

Blessed Be

Peter's consent form was returned with the following message:

'Wow! Quite strange and emotional to see this again after so many years. Thank you for following your instincts. Lovely to hear from you again.

Blessed Be
P....

www.mardibooks.com

Suggested Further Reading

Austen, A.W., The Teachings of Silver Birch,
Two World Publishing Co. Ltd. London.

Duffy, William, Sugar Blues,
ISBN D-446-36181-X.

Gennaro,F.L., Kirlian Photography,
East West Publications, London, ISBN 0-85692 1602.

Lucas, Winafred Blake, Ph.D., Regression Therapy, Volume I and II,
Phoenix Research Publications, London, Deep Forest Press,
ISBN 1-882530-00-4 and 1-88 2530-02-0.

Oldfield, Harry and Coghill, Roger, The Dark Side of the Brain,
Elements Books Ltd., ISBN 1-852 30-025-6.

Rochlitz, Steven, Allergies & Candida, 2nd Edition,
Human Ecology Sciences, Inc., NY., ISBN 0-945 262 -26-4.

Roet, Brian, Dr. Hypnosis, the Gateway to better Health,
J.M. Dent & Sons Ltd. London, ISBN 0-460-12591-5.

Upledger, John,E.,D.O.,Your Inner Physician and You,
North Atlantic Books, California, ISBN 1-55643-246-1.

White, Erica, Beat Candida Cookbook,
ISBN 09521465 09

Woolger, Roger, Ph.D., Other Lives Other Selves,
Thorsons 1994, ISBN 1-855 38-311-X.

You Can't
Hurt Me
Paul King

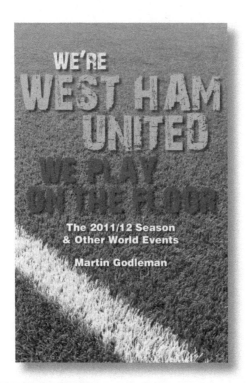